# MEASURES *of* SUCCESS®

## *for string orchestra*

### A Comprehensive Musicianship String Method

**GAIL V. BARNES • BRIAN BALMAGES • CARRIE LANE GRUSELLE • MICHAEL TROWBRIDGE**

## TO THE STUDENT

Congratulations on choosing to play in the orchestra! Orchestras have played an important role throughout history and have performed for kings, queens, presidents, and countless other historical figures. You are about to begin an exciting musical journey full of rewards and performance opportunities. As you practice, you will find yourself sharing the gift of music with family, friends and audiences. So get ready—your path to success begins now!

## ALL-IN-ONE DVD

Your book comes with an All-In-One DVD. It includes tuning notes, instructional videos, and accompaniments for every exercise in the book. You can also put the DVD into your computer to access and transfer the mp3 files to a portable device or burn to a CD. You may also stream or download all videos and recordings by following the instructions on the inside back cover of this book.

## TO THE DIRECTOR

We are proud to introduce you to *Measures of Success® for String Orchestra*. This exciting method engages students in a variety of ways, including playing, listening, composing, evaluating, conducting, and critiquing.

*Measures of Success® for String Orchestra* is divided into four chapters, each referred to as an Opus. This organizational layout creates a balance of short-term and long-term goals for students. Full-page assessments follow each Opus and address critical listening, playing by ear, composing, theory and terminology, performance, and bowing.

As educators know, there is much more to music than learning to play an instrument. By its very nature, music enriches life, builds community, and helps develop an incredible sense of discipline and a strong work ethic. It is no wonder students involved with music statistically perform at higher levels in many other pursuits. It is with this great respect for the power of music that we welcome you to *Measures of Success® for String Orchestra*.

Best wishes for an incredible school year!
*Gail V. Barnes, Brian Balmages, Carrie Lane Gruselle and Michael Trowbridge*

Production: Frank J. Hackinson
Production Coordinators: Brian Balmages and Ken Mattis
Cover Design: Andi Whitmer and Danielle Taylor
Interior Line Drawings: Adrianne Hirosky, Danielle Taylor and Andi Whitmer
Interior Layout and Design: Andi Whitmer and Ken Mattis
Engraving: Tempo Music Press, Inc. / Printer: Tempo Music Press, Inc.

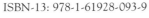

**THE FJH MUSIC COMPANY INC.**
Frank J. Hackinson

ISBN-13: 978-1-61928-093-9

# TABLE OF CONTENTS

# SEQUENCE OF MEASURES OF SUCCESS®

| CONDUCTOR PAGE | 20-21 | 22-29 | 22-29 | 30-32 | 32-35 | 36-40 | 40-44 | 45-50 | 51-55 | 56-58 | 59-61 | 62-67 |
|---|---|---|---|---|---|---|---|---|---|---|---|---|
| STUDENT PAGE | 1 | 2 | 3 | 4 | 5 | 6 | 7 | 8 | 9 | 10 | 11 | 12 |
| **BOWING SKILLS** | | | | | | | | | Bow Workout No. 1: Preparing the Right Hand | Bow Workout No. 2: Moving from the Elbow | Bow-nus: El-Bow | Bow Workout No. 3: Bow Hold / Bow Workout No. 4: Rosin Bowing / From Rosin to String! |
| **THEORY** Fundmental Terminology | | | | Music Staff Bar Line Measure Final Bar Line | 𝄞 𝄡 𝄢 4/4 3/4 Repeat Sign | Accidentals Sharp Natural | | | Ledger Lines: (Viola / Cello / Bass) | Major Scale | | |
| Additional Terminology | | | | Opus Beat Rhythm Pizzicato | | | | | | | | |
| **RHYTHM** | | | | ♩ 𝄽 | | | | | | | | |
| **HISTORY** Music \| Art \| World | Instrument History | | | | | | Beethoven | | | | | |
| **COMPREHENSIVE HIGHLIGHTS** | | Parts of the Instrument / Instrument Care | | | | | | | | Opus 1 Encore! | Opus 1 Encore! | |
| **CLASSICAL MUSIC AND FOLK SONGS** | | | | | | | Don't Tell Aunt Rhody! / Au Claire de la Lune / Ode to Joy | Cold Cross Buns / Groovin' Grandma | Mary Had a Little Lamb | | | |
| **BASS FEATURES** | | | | | | | | III pos. / Meet B! / III...to...I...Lift off! / Preparing Cold Buns / Groovin' Grandpa | French Bow Hold / German Bow Hold / Shifting Gears / Taking III Position | | | Tube Bowing |
| **INSTRUCTIONAL VIDEOS** | | | Holding the Instrument | | | Preparing the Left Hand | | III pos. (Bass) | Bow Workout No. 1: Preparing the Right Hand | Bow Workout No. 2: Moving from the Elbow | | Bow Workout No. 3 / Bow Workout No. 4 / From Rosing to String |
| **NOTE SEQUENCE** | | | | | | | | | | | | |

# FOR STRING ORCHESTRA

| CONDUCTOR PAGE | 67-72 | 72-76 | 77-80 | 81-84 | 84-87 | 88-91 | 92-94 | 95-99 | 100-103 | 104-106 | 107-110 | 111-117 |
|---|---|---|---|---|---|---|---|---|---|---|---|---|
| **STUDENT PAGE** | 13 | 14 | 15 | 16 | 17 | 18 | 19 | 20 | 21 | 22 | 23 | 24 |
| **BOWING SKILLS** | Arm Levels | | | | Retake | | | Bow-nus: *Welcome the Heroes* | | | | Double Stop (Violin / Viola / Cello) | |
| **THEORY** Fundmental Terminology | | | New Key Signature: D Major | | First and Second Endings  Duet | Andante Moderato Allegro | | Round | | | 2/4 Theme and Variations | Common time 𝄴 |
| **Additional Terminology** | | | | | | Tempo | | | | | | |
| **RHYTHM** | | | | 𝅗𝅥 — | | | | | | ♫ | | |
| **HISTORY** Music \| Art \| World | | | | | | Tchaikovsky | | | | | | |
| **COMPREHENSIVE HIGHLIGHTS** | | Left Hand Meets Right Hand | | | Duet: *Two for One* | Duet: *Epic* | Opus 2 Encore | Curtain Up! First Concert  Round: *D Major Scale*  Round: *Love the Sun Defenders of Earth* | Curtain Up! First Concert  Round: *All the Woods are Waking*  *Holidays United!*  *Down on the Farm* | Beam Groups | Conducting in 2/4 time | Left-Hand Pizzicato  4th-finger A (Violin / Viola)  Opt. II pos. (Cello)  Conducting in 4/4 time |
| **CLASSICAL MUSIC AND FOLK SONGS** | | | | *Walking Horses*  *Sleeping Baby* | *Jingle Bells* | *Overture to The Nutcracker* | | *Love the Sun* | *Joy to the World*  *Dreidel Song*  *Old MacDonald* | | *Boil Them Cabbage Down* | *Huron Carol* |
| **BASS FEATURES** | | | | | | | | | | | | III pos. on D String  *Finding G in III*  *I to III and Back on D*  *Déja Vu*  III Position Workouts |
| **INSTRUCTIONAL VIDEOS** | Arm Levels | | | | | | | | | | | |
| **NOTE SEQUENCE** Violin  Viola  Cello  Bass | | | | | | | | | | | | (music notation) |

SB307TM

# SEQUENCE OF MEASURES OF SUCCESS®

| | | | | | | | | | | | | |
|---|---|---|---|---|---|---|---|---|---|---|---|---|
| **CONDUCTOR PAGE** | 118-124 | 125-128 | 129-133 | 134-138 | 139-143 | 144-148 | 149-152 | 153-157 | 158-161 | 162-167 | 168-172 | 172-180 |
| **STUDENT PAGE** | 25 | 26 | 27 | 28 | 29 | 30 | 31 | 32 | 33 | 34 | 35 | 36 |
| **BOWING SKILLS** | | | | | | | Bow-nus: *Serenade for Strings* | | Staccato ♩ | Hooked Bowing | Hooked String Crossings / Slurred String Crossings | |
| **THEORY** Fundmental Terminology | Ledger Lines (Violin) / D.C. al Fine / Double Bar Line | | Upbeats | New Key Signature: G Major | | | Enclosed Repeat Signs ‖: :‖ | | Staccato Dynamics $f$ | | | |
| **Additional Terminology** | | | Maestoso | | | | | | Misterioso | Allegretto | Dolce | Courtesy accidental |
| **RHYTHM** | | | | The Rule of the Dot ♩. | Tie / Slur | | | | | | | |
| **HISTORY** Music \| Art \| World | | | Handel | | | Mahler | | | | Mozart | | |
| **COMPREHENSIVE HIGHLIGHTS** | Round: *Frére Jacques* | Conducting in 3/4 time | | 4th-finger D (Violin / Viola) | | | Opus 3 Encore | Curtain Up! *Fantastic Fiddles* Round: *Do You Hear?* *Preludium* | Duet: *Dueling Cuckoos* | Duet: *Allegretto from Symphony No. 7* | | |
| **CLASSICAL MUSIC AND FOLK SONGS** | *Frére Jaques* / *French Carol* | *Music for the Royal Fireworks* | *Dry Bones* / *Rain, Rain, Go Away* / *Volga Boatmen* / *Chicken on the Fence Post* | *Little Ducklings* | *Three Tied Mice* / *Three Gliding Mice* | *Ode to Joy* Round: *Theme from Symphony No. 1* / *Chester* | *The Moreen* | *Do You Hear?* | | *Allegretto from Symphony No. 7* / *Theme from Sonata No. 11* | *Hush, Little Baby* | |
| **BASS FEATURES** | *Tune This Tune* / II Pos. / *II for You* / *The Matching Game* / *Almost French* | | | | | | | | | II 1/2 pos. / *The B Twins* | | C in II 1/2 and III pos. *Shifting Naturally* / *Blues Etude* / *All Three in III* / *Shifting Gears* / *C from I to III* |
| **INSTRUCTIONAL VIDEOS** | II pos. (Bass) | | | | Slur | | | | Staccato | Hooked Bowing | II 1/2 pos. (Bass) | Low 2nd Finger (Violin / Viola) / C Natural (Cello / Bass) |
| **NOTE SEQUENCE** Violin / Viola / Cello / Bass | (musical notation: II, opt. 2 4) | | | (musical notation: 4) | | | | | | | (opt.) 1 4 — II½ | (opt.) 2 1 — II½ III |

# FOR STRING ORCHESTRA

| | 181-188 | 189-193 | 194-198 | 198-203 | 204-207 | 208-211 | 212-215 | 216-221 | 222-226 | 227-230 | 231-235 | 236-239 |
|---|---|---|---|---|---|---|---|---|---|---|---|---|
| **CONDUCTOR PAGE** | | | | | | | | | | | | |
| **STUDENT PAGE** | 37 | 38 | 39 | 40 | 41 | 42 | 43 | 44 | 45 | 46 | 47 | 48 |
| **BOWING SKILLS** | | | | | | | | | | | | |
| **THEORY** Fundmental Terminology | Intervals Half Step Whole Step | | New Key Signature: C Major | | | Crescendo Decrescendo | | | | | | |
| **Additional Terminology** | Octave | Pesante | | | | | Improvisation | | | | | |
| **RHYTHM** | | | | Whole Rest | | o | | | | | | |
| **HISTORY** Music \| Art \| World | | | | | Schubert | Chopin | | | | | | |
| **COMPREHENSIVE HIGHLIGHTS** | | | | 4th-Finger G (Viola) | 4th-Finger E (Violin / Viola) | | Opus 4 Encore | Curtain Up! Can-Can | Curtain Up! Power and Pulse | Instrumental Solo with Piano Accompaniment | Scales and Arpeggios Fingering Chart | Index |
| **CLASSICAL MUSIC AND FOLK SONGS** | Yankee Doodle La Morisque Los Pollitos | Snake Chant | Shepherd's Hey Country Gardens The Man on the Flying Trapeze Theme from Hansel and Gretel Flower Drum Song | A-Tisket, A-Tasket | Marche Militaire Turkish March | Concerto Theme Fantaisie-Impromptu | The Great Gate of Kiev | Can-Can | | | | |
| **BASS FEATURES** | Closer Than You Think Speed Shifting Sliding Down Piece of Cake | | | | | | | | | | Scale Studies Position Studies | |
| **INSTRUCTIONAL VIDEOS** | | | | | | | | | | | | |
| **NOTE SEQUENCE** | | | | | | | | | | | | |

# HOW TO USE THE TEACHER'S MANUAL

*Measures of Success® for String Orchestra* is a comprehensive musicianship string method that includes a wealth of teaching opportunities including ideas to incorporate the National Standards for Music Education. There are several key elements throughout the book.

## ORGANIZATION: THE OPUS SYSTEM

The authors organized the book into four chapters labeled Opus 1 through 4. Each Opus begins with the introduction of new concepts and the reinforcement of concepts learned in the previous Opus. We designed the book for each Opus to last approximately one quarter of a grading period, though some classes will move slower or faster depending on contact time and developmental level.

## ASSESSMENT

While there are numerous opportunities for assessment throughout the method, there is an *Encore!* page at the end of each Opus in which we provide a variety of assessments based on chapter content. Students can do many of these assessments in class or at home, or even with a substitute teacher who may not have formal music training. They include the following:

- **Interpretation Station** (critical listening): Students listen to musical examples and are asked to critique performances, identify style / tempo markings, time signatures and more.

- **Simon Sez** (playing by ear): Students listen to patterns and echo them back. Eventually, students are given basic tunes and are asked to learn / play them by ear. These exercises always use notes that students have already learned.

- **Composer's Corner** (composition, arranging and improvisation): Progressive lessons move from composition into basic arranging and early improvisation.

- **Pencil Power** (theory and terminology): Written exercises reinforce everything from terms and notation to composers and historical facts.

- **Curtain Up!** (performance): Musical exercises assess what students have learned in the Opus.

- **Bow-nus!** (special bow exercises): Studies enrich, supplement and further develop right-hand technique.

Remember that you do not have to perform a "Curtain Up!" piece to program a fun and successful concert. Any number of pieces and exercises in the book can be used as concert pieces, alone, with the recorded accompaniments or with piano accompaniment. Creative arranging of tunes can lead to medleys, combinations of small groups, soloists and the full ensemble performing different phrases. Play arco, then pizzicato – the possibilities are endless. Students can help determine the concert pieces and create their own program!

## ENSEMBLE PERFORMANCE

Beginning with Opus 2, every chapter includes string orchestra performance music (eight string orchestra pieces total). Opus 2 in particular offers a collection of pieces ideal for a first performance. It includes a warm-up scale, a round, and 4 performance pieces that can be performed by a complete string orchestra or as a duet. All orchestra arrangements include A, B and C parts and are presented in the form of duets in each student book.

A = melody (included for all instruments)
B = harmony (violin and viola)
C = bass line (cello and bass)

## MUSIC THEORY

Important concepts in music theory related to performance and overall musicianship are placed sequentially. After being introduced, concepts are highlighted in exercises that follow.

## RHYTHM

Rhythm boxes introduce new rhythmic concepts and are always followed by an exercise that reinforces the concept. Often, these concepts are further reinforced with Bow Beat exercises, in which students rosin or tube bow prior to playing on the instrument.

## HISTORY (MUSIC, SCIENCE, AND WORLD)

In addition to performance and technique concepts, each Opus contains historical information that places simultaneous music, science, and world events side-by-side so students get a sense of what was happening in the world when certain musical works were being composed and performed.

## VIDEOS

Video icons are presented throughout the book and indicate that there is an instructional video available for the skill being presented in the book. These videos feature master teachers working with younger students in a real world environment.

## ACCOMPANIMENT

All accompaniment tracks are available on the All-in-One DVD that comes with each book. These can either be accessed using a DVD player or by inserting the DVD into a computer to access the mp3 files. In addition, they can be accessed online by using the authentication code printed in the back inside cover of each book. Each accompaniment includes a demonstration track with professional musicians followed by the accompaniment alone. These are great motivational tools and cover a wide variety of musical styles to make practice exciting and fun.

## BASS BOOK FEATURES

The bass book contains 8 additional pages of material to supplement what students are learning in a heterogeneous environment. While bass players can be successful using I and III position only, we also introduce II and II$^{1/2}$ where it makes shifting easier and also makes it possible to avoid shifting during a slur. The numerous supplemental exercises make it easy to learn new positions and practice shifting. Studies include:

- Special Studies for Bass: Reinforcing III position and shifting
- Third Position Workouts: Reinforcing III position on G and D strings
- Second Position Workouts: Introducing and reinforcing II position
- Scale Studies: Technique studies based on scales presented in the method
- Position Studies: Four sections of studies that reinforce shifting to various positions and can be used to supplement as needed

## SCALES AND ARPEGGIOS

Students are given scales without specific time signatures so teachers can choose a different rhythmic pattern each time. Dotted bar lines separate the scale into the ascending pattern, descending pattern, and arpeggio.

## MEASURING FOR SUCCESS

In the beginning stages, the process of playing the instrument with correct position is more important than how the student sounds. Some young players with poor fundamentals may be able to sound good on easy tunes. This is only temporary. Once the student is learning Grade 3 music (requiring shifting and more advanced bow techniques), poor habits result in poor execution, intonation and tone. In this introduction, we hope to help remind both teachers and students about the importance of keeping fundamentals at the forefront in the early learning stages and reviewing these skills daily.

### VIOLIN AND VIOLA

To ensure the violin or viola is a correct length for the student to achieve success and play in tune, here are a few simple guidelines:

- With the instrument sitting properly on the shoulder/collarbone and supported by the right hand or the teacher, reach the left arm out to the scroll. The student should be able to curl the fingers all the way around the scroll without straining or stretching.

- Look for ample room (several inches) between the back of the violin and the inside of the student's elbow. That space provides relaxation room for the arm and a comfortable position to stretch the fingers in whole steps, and later, shifting and vibrato.

- Check to see if the hand is large enough (or the instrument short enough) for the 2nd finger to pull away from the 1st in order to make the whole step E to F♯ on the D string. Direct attention to the illustrations on pages 6 and 8 of the student method book.

- Give the students brief information on where to pluck the string for the best pizzicato sound in both guitar and shoulder position. Give them permission to experiment with the distance from the bridge that produces the best sound. This could open up an opportunity to discuss the need for short fingernails.

### CELLO AND BASS

To ensure the cello and bass are the correct size, height and angle, refer to the information on page 3 of the student books. There are many tips for students and teachers to guarantee student success by being absolutely certain that each student understands how high the instrument should be, the correct angle, points of contact and pizzicato technique. This information can also be found in the Teacher's Manual on pages 26-29.

### RECRUITMENT

Most students will recognize a violin but may not be aware of the difference between a violin and a viola, cello and bass. When recruiting, it is important that you provide a model of the characteristic sound of each instrument. Below are a few thoughts on recruitment.

- If you seem to be getting an exceptionally high number of violins in your classes, be sure to place more emphasis on viola, cello or bass. It is always effective to bring in a group of middle or high school students to play for the future string students. Have them dress casually and emphasize their "cool" factor.

- You do not need to model virtuoso playing. It is actually more effective to model a simple folk tune or recognizable popular tune. This will get the students' attention and engage their imaginations.

- Play the same tune on each instrument and draw attention to the differences.

- Be visible in your school. Even if you do not play concerts frequently, have your students play happy birthday to teachers and administrators or play "dinner music" in the lunchroom! Another idea is to serenade the office staff with holiday music at various times of the year.

- When waiting for your class, stand in the hall with a violin or viola and chat with younger children while waiting for your next class to arrive.

## RETAINMENT

Once students have signed up for orchestra, the focus should shift to effective and positive instruction and methods to retain students. Consider the following:

- Without being discouraging, emphasize that learning a stringed instrument is an exciting journey that lasts more than a single year. Let students know you are looking forward to seeing them play next year, in middle school and on to high school. Drop-in performances from high school students are an ideal way to excite students. In addition, there is great value in side-by-side performances. Older students get to come back and mentor beginners, while beginning students get to sound more mature and see many techniques modeled by older students.

- There often comes a time when the novelty of playing a string instrument has worn off. Teachers need to be aware that this is a normal phase to work through, and should spend time coming up with ways to make it fun (suggestions occur throughout the Teacher's Manual).

- Dorothy Straub (AST, Autumn, 1985) very wisely said that kids ask themselves two questions when deciding whether to stay with a stringed instrument: "Do I like it?" and "Am I good at it?" We have to make sure they answer yes to both questions!

- No teacher has a 100% retention rate every year, but start analyzing the situation if attrition is more than 5-10%. You may have a higher rate of attrition if your school or district has a high degree of transience, but do track those students to help them find a home in a string class in another school. Communication with other directors is key.

- String teachers tend to work with their students for consecutive years; thus, it can be easy to take it personally if they decide not to continue. It is the opinion of the authors that every student deserves to be asked to stay. Even if they do not stay, consider what you want them to remember in ten or twenty years – that someone wanted them to keep playing a stringed instrument. That person may be more likely to subscribe to their local symphony or even to start playing again as an adult.

- We cannot always control the few children that sign up for strings and switch to band. This can be influenced by their family traditions and what their parents or older siblings did. Optimally, you have a great relationship with your band colleague so there is not a great number that switch. If they do, wish them well and stay positive. Their future attitude toward orchestra and their class mates in orchestra can be shaped by how you handle this.

- Remember: The best recruitment and retention tool is a successful experience for your students!

## CLASS SET-UP, MANAGEMENT, AND MOVING AROUND THE ROOM

- Keep bass players close to you in front of class so that they are not forgotten in the back of the room. In tight quarters, this also helps you be able to give them necessary feedback more easily.

- Sitting or standing (violin, viola and bass)
  - One of the best options might be to do a mixture of standing and sitting. Chairs will give students a home base and a place to sit when they need a break from working hard on proper standing position!
  - When students are sitting, you can keep them from wandering and roaming around the classroom.
  - When standing, students will develop fewer bad habits in posture. This is also useful if you do not have a dedicated classroom. Set-up is faster if you need fewer chairs.

- Traditional orchestra seating does not work well with beginning students. Setting up the class in rows so that you can walk and move around the class is useful and you will be able to reach every student to help with posture, left-hand position and bow hold.

- You may choose to play piano on accompaniments as a treat, but you will spend most of the class time circulating and adjusting left and right-hand positions during the critical early stages. The recorded accompaniments are a great option if you want to circulate while students play along with a background track.

- Another method that allows you to move around the room involves a system of disguised repetition, or what Dillon & Kriechbaum called a self-propelling class. (Jacquelyn Dillon-Krass and Casimer B. Kriechbaum, Jr., *How to Design and Teach a Successful School String and Orchestra Program,* [San Diego: Kjos West, 1978], pp. 79-80)

  - The whole class plays the line (either bowing or playing pizzicato) while also singing the note names and rests.

  - Without stopping, the line is repeated by row 1 (playing and singing) while the rest of the class sings the notes and rests without playing.

  - Without stopping, the whole class plays and sings the line together again.

  - Continue with row 2, row 3, etc.

  - As students progress, you can add activities for those who are only singing, such as fingering along or playing pizzicato while others bow.

  - Eventually the students get the routine and the teacher is free to move about the classroom, adjusting posture, pointing to the spot in the music, etc.

- Students tend to like the pieces they already know and they have a *much* greater capacity for repetition than adults. Pace your class so that you start with something familiar, put the new material in the middle and then end with a class favorite. Students will remember these first pieces with fondness and some will play them into high school! Also, if they become string teachers themselves, these will frequently be the pieces they want to teach!

## ISOLATING RIGHT AND LEFT-HAND SKILL DEVELOPMENT

Many beginning string class teachers initially have students pluck the string *(pizzicato)* so they can focus on left-hand skill development. In the case of violin and viola, students often learn to pluck initial tunes in guitar position. This and shoulder position are explained on page 3 of the student books. As guitar position involves only plucking with the right thumb (a skill that requires little instruction and practice), teachers can spend time on left-hand skills and beginning music reading. Regardless of the string instrument, it is important to gradually introduce right-hand skills separately from the left hand (as suggested in the book). Working on the right and left hand separately helps reinforce those skills. Right hand and music reading skills benefit in the same way. If they are learned separately, they can be layered on or combined more easily.

## CREATING A STRONG FOUNDATION FOR THE LEFT HAND

### TO TAPE OR NOT TAPE...
String teachers can have long conversations about tape (or other markers) on fingerboards. While each teacher needs to decide what works best in his or her situation, here are a few suggestions:

- Use materials that will eventually wear off.

- Be aware of materials that slip on the fingerboard, making the aid inaccurate.

- Start with the interval of a fourth on violin, viola and cello (G on D, D on A) and the interval of a third (F♯ on D) on the string bass.

- If you place a 'thumb house' (corn pad) on the neck for violin and viola, this is a good landmark for 1st finger. Thumb houses for cello and bass go behind the 2nd finger.

- If a student is struggling with finding pitches, add markers as necessary. It is important for the student to be successful and not feel frustration.

- After a few weeks, encourage students not to look at their hand, perhaps using games in which they close their eyes and realize they *do* know where their fingers go!

## HAND POSITION AND PLACEMENT

From the outset, encourage students to keep all fingers curved and hovering above the string, even when they are not being used. Students often want to curl up 3rd and 4th fingers when they are not pushing down the string. Always reinforce this and have students check their own finger position and look at a partner as well. We remind students throughout the method that their fingers should hover over the string, even when not being used.

Impress on the students the need to keep all left-hand fingers well rounded and curved. Curved fingers are stronger than flat fingers and string players need strong fingers! A quick model of a fist compared to a flat, shapeless hand will make a strong visual and kinetic impression. Also show that curved fingers are very flexible at all the joints and can move extremely fast compared to flat fingers.

## THE THUMB (VIOLIN AND VIOLA)

- Point the thumb at the ceiling or possibly at a small angle. If the thumb straightens out and leans back toward the bottom of the scroll, this will start a trend that may end up with a "flat wrist," which should be avoided at all costs. Students with short thumbs may set the neck lower into the web between thumb and 1st finger to allow the latter to form that squared-off position that is so important to skills needed later. Do not let the tip of the thumb protrude above the fingerboard.

- Thumb placement: While one can find differences in thumb placement among skilled violinists, placing the pad of the thumb opposite the first finger is optimal for beginners. For example, it will facilitate later skills (especially shifting to higher positions).

## THE THUMB (CELLO AND BASS)

- The thumb should be parallel to the floor and behind the 2nd finger.

- Model how the thumb touches the center of the back of the neck, but explain how it NEVER squeezes the neck. Tension is the enemy!

## THE HAND AND WRIST (VIOLIN AND VIOLA)

- Explain and model a straight wrist. Students need to understand that a straight, yet relaxed wrist is stronger and more flexible than a bent, collapsed wrist (just the opposite of the fingers).

- We often tell students to keep the elbow "under" the instrument. Actually, we often need the elbow to swing farther to the right of the middle of the instrument and a little closer to the player's belly button (e.g. when students are getting ready to use 3rd and 4th fingers). Another example is when they play on the lower strings, where a pull of the elbow to the right, coupled with a slight rotation of the wrist to the left, moves the 3rd and 4th fingers farther to the left, setting those fingertips in just the right place over the lower strings. Lead the class in modeling this pull of the elbow to the right while rotating the wrist slightly to the left without the instrument. When they are ready, do the same motion with the instrument in place, supported by the right hand if necessary.

## THE HAND AND WRIST (CELLO AND BASS)

- The hand should make a C shape, as though students are holding a glass of water.

- Fingers should be arched over the strings (reinforce that fingers should hover over the string, even when they are not being used!).

- The left elbow should be raised just enough so that there is a straight line from the back of the hand to the elbow.

- As with violin and viola, students need to understand that a straight, yet relaxed wrist is one of the most important foundations for left-hand technique. Check it often and correct as necessary.

## CREATING A STRONG FOUNDATION FOR THE RIGHT HAND

Many teachers prefer to introduce the bow hold away from the bow using an unsharpened pencil. If you prefer to teach the bow hold using the bow itself, have students do so at the balance point, where the bow is much lighter and easier to control. Once learned, it is a simple matter to transfer the bow hold to the frog.

This method systematically develops the right hand through Bow Workouts.

- *Bow Workout No. 1: Preparing the Right Hand.* Students learn to form a bow hold on the pencil and are encouraged to keep fingers flexible.

- *Bow Workout No. 2: Moving from the Elbow.* The basic bowing motion is introduced while still using a pencil. Emphasis is placed on which part(s) of the arm move when bowing.

- *Bow Workout No. 3: Bow Hold.* Students learn to transfer their bow hold to an actual bow. Many teachers will choose to start with the early bow hold where the hand is placed at the balance point of the bow. The teacher can decide when they are ready to move to the frog.

- *Bow Workout No. 4: Rosin and Tube Bowing.* Violin, viola and cello students practice bowing on rosin. It is suggested that violinists and violists hold the rosin by their left shoulder. This encourages movement from the right elbow when bowing. Cellists should place the rosin in front of them at waist level and parallel to the floor. Bassists have two options. Since bass rosin is very sticky, they are only able to practice down bows; however, this is still an important skill as they need to be able to rosin their bows. Tube bowing is also recommended, where the student places the bow in a tube (PVC, toilet paper, etc.) to practice the correct bowing motion.

A big word of warning: The term "tip" of the two outer fingers – thumb and pinkie – has wide interpretation. Many students assume that the PAD of those fingers is the tip. Stress and reinforce that the TIP is out at the very end of the finger at the fingernails, which should be clipped quite short. If the students begin to play with the outer fingers on their pads, those fingers will collapse almost instantly, and they will be bowing with flat fingers. Refer everybody to the drawings often. Flat outer fingers will cause a host of issues down the road, so it is best to stay on top of this from the very beginning.

While students should practice the Bow Workouts every day, it is important that they do not practice at home with the bow until they have established good habits in the classroom. Sarah Black (Gwinnett County, Georgia) gave us the idea of a License to Bow. Students are not allowed to play with the bow at home until they get their license! You can present this License at their first performance with great ceremony.

## TUNING

- With a large class and a short class period, even a veteran teacher could spend most of the class tuning. Some teachers opt to tune only the D and A strings in beginning classes. One can argue the instrument is not truly in tune unless the sympathetic vibrations are set properly, but reality can influence what is practical.

- Keeping students busy during tuning is a classroom management issue. Some ideas:
    - Kids play solos (one at a time) while the teacher quietly tunes instruments.
    - Students can line up and show the teacher their bow holds while the teacher tunes the instruments.
    - After students start using the bow, you can tune one and have him/her play the A string. After a couple of students are tuned, they can play their D strings. This reinforces the perfect 5th and facilitates them learning to tune their own instruments in the future.

## EAR TRAINING

- Playing short melodic patterns for students to echo is another important aspect of developing their ears.

- You can use pizzicato or arco. Use open strings at first and then add the notes they are learning. Playing short fragments of four quarter notes can help all students feel success. Note that the *Simon Sez* portion of the Opus 1 and 2 assessments address this concept.

- Changing strings unannounced makes a good beginning ear-training exercise. Later, fingerings, other rhythmic patterns and bowing can be added; even dynamics. Simply say "Do as I do," and students will follow your lead!

- When doing echo work, be sure to vary the bowing style.

## SINGING

- Encourage students to sing from the very beginning. We give reminders in specific exercises but we could have said it for every single exercise because it is that important! We have witnessed students be able to actually sight sing a melody before they play or hear it when they have been trained to sing from the very beginning stages.

- Students can internalize the interval of a 5th in the pre-left hand stages by singing the "Ant Song" (students can pluck the corresponding open strings on the half notes while singing):

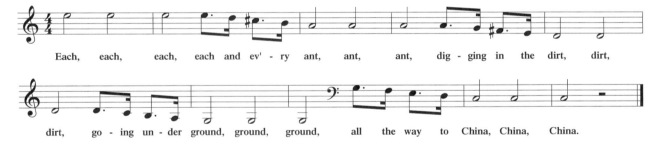

- Another tool in developing the ear and a sense of musical style is to play recordings frequently. You may choose to play a simple song such as *Chicken on the Fence Post* (3.28). or *March Militaire* (4.40) as they enter the class. The students may surprise you by starting to sing it when they hear it, making it easier when you introduce it in the future.

## MODELING (INCLUDING SILENT MODELING)

- Modeling is one of the most important teaching techniques in any string teacher's bag of tricks. Even non-string players need to model at a basic level and on each instrument.

- Silent Modeling: There are times when a silent demonstration of a position or movement can be a very effective teaching tool, perhaps *even better* than an excellent demonstration on an instrument. Can this really be true? Yes! The silent (or mostly silent) model tends to focus the students' attention on the one individual skill the teacher is developing. A full demonstration may give the young beginner too many areas of playing to focus on. The student is distracted by the shape of the tune, its beauty or excitement, the quality of the teacher's playing, including tone rich in vibrato and volume, the teacher's body language, bowing and other movements that are important but not the subject of the skill under discussion. In other words, a well-timed (usually very short) demonstration of hand and finger positions draws and keeps the students' attention on that one particular skill under development. Often, no words, or only a few, need be spoken. A clear picture – here in 3D – can be worth a thousand words!

## PRACTICING

Students do not tend to respond well when teachers simply tell them to practice, so it is important to come up with a system that is rewarding and fun. Each student book contains a practice log ("Measuring Our Success!") where students can keep track of their practice time and assignments. In addition, teachers should consider supplementing in fun ways. For example, students earn their white belt with good sitting or standing position. They can earn their yellow belt with good left-hand position. Have awards for those who become a black belt!

Another important suggestion (attributed to Bob Duke, University of Texas at Austin) is to tell students they are not allowed to practice outside of class until you give them permission. This is actually a good idea so they do not learn bad habits. When they are ready, you give them permission to practice five minutes *only*. Eventually they are allowed to practice for ten minutes and so on. Once everyone has the hang of it, make it fun and tell them to only practice on the days they eat! (Thanks, Dr. Suzuki!)

## ELEMENTS OF A HEALTHY ORCHESTRA PROGRAM

Teachers often believe that an ideal orchestra program is one with a beautiful, new facility filled with a supportive administration and colleagues. While many teachers may be working in a less than ideal physical setting, it is still possible to create and develop this support. Ask yourself if you are doing everything you can to create the Pillars of a Healthy Orchestra Program (Robert Gillespie and Donald Hamman, *Strategies for Teaching Strings: Building a Successful String and Orchestra Program,* Third Edition [Oxford University Press, 2012], pp. 151-156).

Do you inform those in power about the values of orchestra programs?
- The music curriculum is not complete without the orchestra.
- The school orchestra increases the value of a school district.
- School orchestra programs benefit students.

Do you do everything you can to be a good string teacher?
- Do you find resources on the web?
- Do you go to conferences and workshops to keep refining your skills?

Do you know where model programs are and do your best to emulate them?
- Remember, directors in highly visible programs work *hard*. There are no easy jobs, but directors who work diligently for their students generally find it very fulfilling.

Do you keep data and use research *appropriately* to advocate for your program?
- Having great organizational skills is a must!

Do you use your stakeholders (parents, community) effectively?

Finally, do you do everything you can to ensure a motivated student is able to participate? This may mean enlisting support for transportation, finding access to an instrument, and working with your guidance department to clear scheduling snags. Being in a string program must not be limited to those with means. As our country becomes increasingly diverse, so should our music programs.

## RECAP IN PRAISE OF FUNDAMENTALS

Experienced string players and teachers (class or private) understand the incredible importance of learning and reviewing the fundamentals that are introduced and stressed in this method book. Less experienced teachers need to learn how valuable – indeed essential – these basic positions, postures and motions are to enable the beginner to advance to a higher level of playing. Fingers not in place over the string will prevent rapid passages from being played cleanly. A left elbow hanging too far to the left will result in sloppy playing on the lower two strings. A wrist that folds in will later inhibit more advanced skills like shifting, playing in the upper positions, and making a beautiful vibrato. A right hand thumb or pinkie that is not curved or on its tip will prevent smooth bow changes, produce thin tone quality by keeping the bow sliding on the surface of the string with no leverage, prevent crisp hooked bows, and more. A diligent and watchful teacher can help students avoid the frustration of later remediation by being vigilant to these common problems. This does not have to be arduous. Look for resources that help you make learning good string playing habits fun!

## REFERENCES

Dillon-Krass, J., & Kriechbaum C. B. (1978). How to Design and Teach a Successful String and
Orchestra Program. San Diego: Kjos West.

Hamann, D. L. & Gillespie, R. (2012). Strategies for Teaching Strings: Building a Successful
String and Orchestra Program, Third Edition. New York: Oxford University Press

Straub, D. (1985) Instrumental Lessons – Designed for Success. American String Teacher,
Autumn, 1985.

## ACKNOWLEDGEMENTS:

Illustration and video models:
Caleb Coker, Ryan Gary, Elaine Geniesse, Carrie Lane Gruselle, Kristen Harris, Katie Holaway, Katie Lindler, Debbie Trowbridge, Michael Trowbridge, and Aidan Ziemba.

The children of the University of South Carolina String Project.

Gregory L. Barnes for his many contributions to the Teacher's Manual.

Meredith Miller for her special way of teaching violin and viola position.

The following teachers who reviewed the method in its development stages:
Lisa Balmages, Gregory Barnes, Ben Bernstein, Sarah Black, Benjamin Denne, Patti L. Gmeiner, Craig Kearns, Cheryl Konkol-Broullire, David Pope, Debbie Trowbridge, Bonnie Zeitlier and the students of the University of South Carolina String Methods Class.

# INSTRUMENT HISTORIES

## HISTORY OF THE VIOLIN

The violin is a member of the string family, which also includes the viola, violoncello and double bass. Its early ancestors were the fiddle and the rebec (a European instrument that was derived from an Arabic stringed instrument dating back to the 8th century!). There are stringed instruments all over the world that are used in many cultures. Some of them are plucked while others are also played with the bow.

The violin we know today was perfected in Italy during the 16th century. The most famous maker from that time is Antonio Stradivari. There are about 600 of his violins still in existence today, and some are worth well over a million dollars!

Composers throughout history have written music for the violin, which can be used to play many types of music including jazz, classical, rock, and fiddle music. Famous violinists include Itzhak Perlman, Jascha Heifetz, Niccolò Paganini, Joshua Bell, Hilary Hahn, and Jean-Luc Ponty.

## HISTORY OF THE VIOLA

The viola is a member of the string family, which also includes the violin, violoncello and double bass. The viola is similar in shape to the violin but is larger. The early ancestors of the violin and viola were the fiddle and the rebec (a European instrument that was derived from an Arabic stringed instrument dating back to the 8th century!). There are stringed instruments all over the world that are used in many cultures. Some of them are plucked while others are also played with the bow.

The viola has a unique voice, similar to the alto voice in a choir. Its range is lower than the violin and higher than the cello.

Many famous composers such as Bach, Beethoven, Dvořák and Haydn played the viola because of its unique sound. Famous viola performers include William Primrose, Yuri Bashmet, Kim Kashkashian and Nokuthula Ngwenyama.

Violin
Ancestors - fiddle, rebec
Italy - 16th century developed
Most famous violin maker - Stradiveri - still makes them today
jazz, classical, rock, fiddle
Paganini, Joshua Bell

# HISTORY OF THE CELLO

The cello, officially called the "violoncello," is a member of the string family, which also includes the violin, viola and double bass. Its earliest ancestors were the fiddle and the rebec (a European instrument that was derived from an Arabic stringed instrument dating back to the 8th century!). There are stringed instruments all over the world that are used in many cultures. Some are plucked while others are also played with the bow.

By the 18th century, the cello's popularity exceeded that of its 16th century predecessors including the viola da gamba and viola da braccio. Although 17th century violin maker Antonio Stradivari is mostly known for his amazing violins, he made many amazing cellos (or celli, to use the correct Italian grammar!)

Composers throughout history have written music for the cello, which can be used to play many types of music including jazz, classical, rock and fiddle music. Famous cellists include Luigi Boccherini, Pablo Casals, Mstislav Rostropovich, Jacqueline du Pré, and Yo-Yo Ma.

# HISTORY OF THE DOUBLE BASS

The bass, officially called the "double bass," is a member of the string family, which also includes the violin, viola and cello. There is some argument about its origin, but it is believed to have originated in 15th or 16th century Europe. As a member of the string family, its earliest ancestors were the fiddle and the rebec (a European instrument that was derived from an Arabic stringed instrument dating back to the 8th century!). There are stringed instruments all over the world that are used in many cultures. Some are plucked while others are also played with the bow.

The double bass is the lowest sounding of all the string instruments, yet it is extremely versatile. Historically, it has used anywhere from 3-6 strings and has changed a great deal over time. Most basses use 4 strings, while professional basses may have 5 strings. Composers throughout history have written music for the bass, which can be used to play many types of music including jazz, classical, rock and bluegrass. Famous players include Franz Simandl, Giovanni Bottesini, Domenico Dragonetti, Hal Robinson, Francois Rabbath, Ron Carter, Rufus Reid, Jaco Pastorius and Christian McBride.

2

# PARTS OF THE VIOLIN AND BOW

## PRACTICE GOOD INSTRUMENT CARE!

### VIOLIN

1. Always handle your instrument with care and avoid extreme temperatures. It can easily be damaged.

2. Your teacher will show you a safe way to remove the instrument from the case and return it.

3. Wipe the instrument clean with a soft cloth.

4. Always remove the shoulder rest before placing the instrument back in the case.

### BOW

1. Your teacher will show you how to remove the bow, tighten the bow hair and apply rosin.

2. Always loosen the bow hair before putting the bow away.

### SUPPLIES

• rosin
• soft cloth
• shoulder rest
• extra set of strings

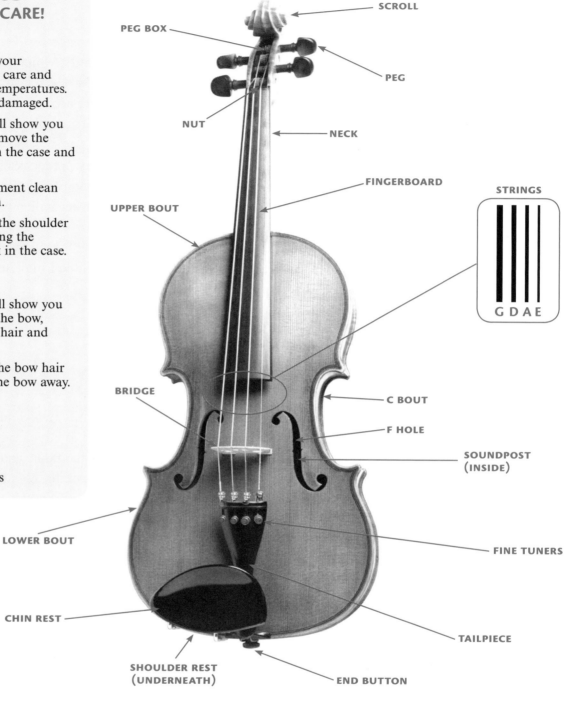

SCROLL
PEG BOX
PEG
NUT
NECK
FINGERBOARD
STRINGS
G D A E
UPPER BOUT
BRIDGE
C BOUT
F HOLE
SOUNDPOST (INSIDE)
LOWER BOUT
FINE TUNERS
CHIN REST
TAILPIECE
SHOULDER REST (UNDERNEATH)
END BUTTON

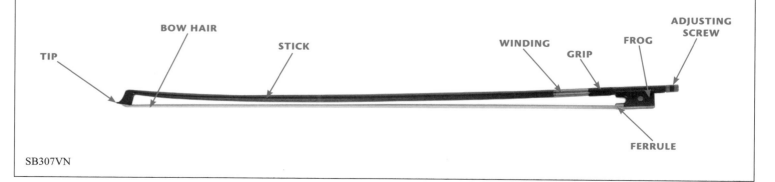

TIP
BOW HAIR
STICK
WINDING
GRIP
FROG
ADJUSTING SCREW
FERRULE

SB307VN

# HOLDING THE INSTRUMENT

3

**Your teacher will determine whether you will start in guitar position or shoulder position. Listen carefully as your teacher explains the proper steps to hold the instrument correctly.**

## GUITAR POSITION

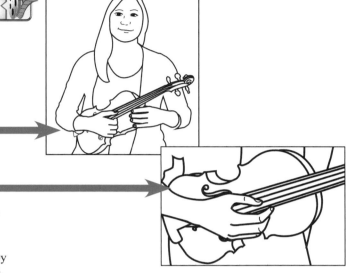

**STEP 1** Place your case on the floor on the left side of your chair. Make sure the curved side is facing up. Carefully remove your instrument.

**STEP 2** Hold the violin flat against your stomach with the scroll to your left. The neck and scroll should be at an angle similar to the illustration. Check the position of your left hand (on the upper bout).

**STEP 3** Move your right thumb over the strings while you place your other fingers under the fingerboard.

**STEP 4** Identify the strings. Moving from top to bottom, the open strings are G (lowest pitch), D, A and E.

**STEP 5** Pluck each string with your right thumb as instructed by your teacher. Plucking is also called *pizzicato* (*pizz.*).

## SHOULDER POSITION

A shoulder rest is essential when holding the instrument in shoulder position. There are many types to choose from, or your teacher may recommend a specific brand.

**STEP 1** Place your case on the floor on the left side of your chair. Make sure the curved side is facing up. Carefully remove your instrument.

**STEP 2** **Statue of Liberty** - Place your left hand on the upper bout and support the bottom of your violin with the right hand. Hold your instrument directly in front of you with the scroll up.

**STEP 3** **Upside down** - Turn your scroll counterclockwise so the scroll is facing down.

**STEP 4** **Flat to the ground** - Lift the scroll so the instrument is parallel to the ground at shoulder level.

**STEP 5** **Bring it in** - Keeping the instrument parallel to the ground, tuck the instrument under your jaw and on top of your collarbone.

**STEP 6** Identify the strings. Moving from your left to right, the open strings are G (lowest pitch), D, A and E.

**STEP 7** Pluck each string with your right-hand 1st finger as instructed by your teacher. Plucking is also called *pizzicato* (*pizz.*).

*Statue of Liberty*

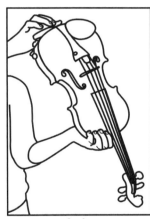

*upside down*

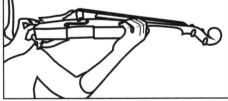

*flat to the ground*

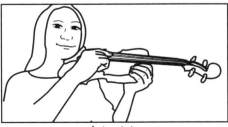

*bring it in*

SB307VN

SB307TM

# PARTS OF THE VIOLA AND BOW

## PRACTICE GOOD INSTRUMENT CARE!

### VIOLA

1. Always handle your instrument with care and avoid extreme temperatures. It can easily be damaged.

2. Your teacher will show you a safe way to remove the instrument from the case and return it.

3. Wipe the instrument clean with a soft cloth.

4. Always remove the shoulder rest before placing the instrument back in the case.

### BOW

1. Your teacher will show you how to remove the bow, tighten the bow hair and apply rosin.

2. Always loosen the bow hair before putting the bow away.

### SUPPLIES

• rosin
• soft cloth
• shoulder rest
• extra set of strings

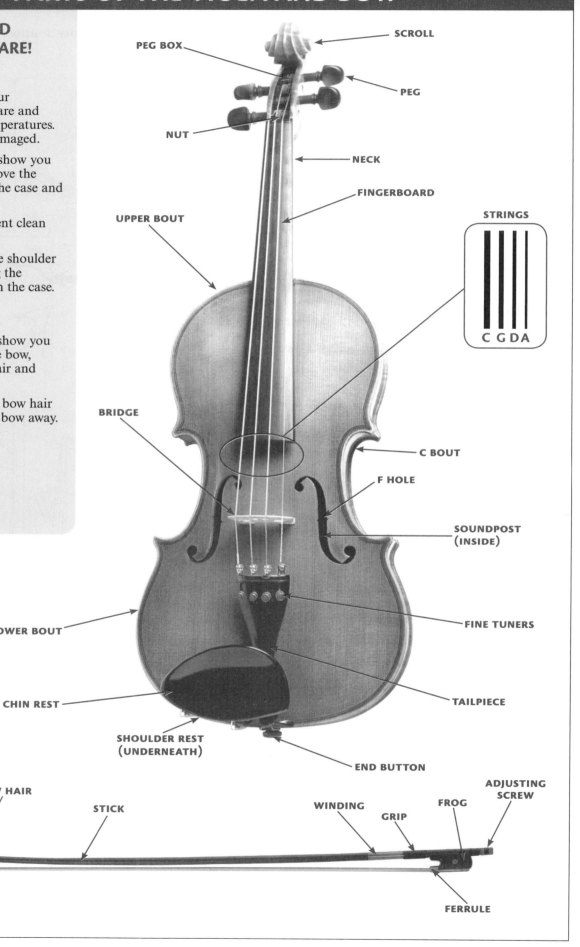

SCROLL

PEG BOX

PEG

NUT

NECK

FINGERBOARD

UPPER BOUT

STRINGS

C G D A

BRIDGE

C BOUT

F HOLE

SOUNDPOST (INSIDE)

FINE TUNERS

LOWER BOUT

CHIN REST

TAILPIECE

SHOULDER REST (UNDERNEATH)

END BUTTON

BOW HAIR

STICK

WINDING

GRIP

FROG

ADJUSTING SCREW

TIP

FERRULE

# HOLDING THE INSTRUMENT

**Your teacher will determine whether you will start in guitar position or shoulder position. Listen carefully as your teacher explains the proper steps to hold the instrument correctly.**

## GUITAR POSITION

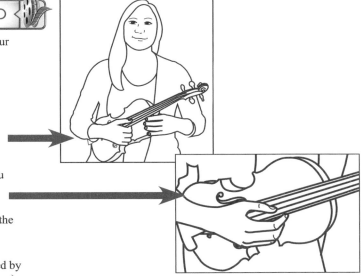

**STEP 1**    Place your case on the floor on the left side of your chair. Make sure the curved side is facing up. Carefully remove your instrument.

**STEP 2**    Hold the viola flat against your stomach with the scroll to your left. The neck and scroll should be at an angle similar to the illustration. Check the position of your left hand (on the upper bout).

**STEP 3**    Move your right thumb over the strings while you place your other fingers under the fingerboard.

**STEP 4**    Identify the strings. Moving from top to bottom, the open strings are C (lowest pitch), G, D and A.

**STEP 5**    Pluck each string with your right thumb as instructed by your teacher. Plucking is also called *pizzicato* (*pizz.*).

## SHOULDER POSITION

A shoulder rest is essential when holding the instrument in shoulder position. There are many types to choose from, or your teacher may recommend a specific brand.

**STEP 1**    Place your case on the floor on the left side of your chair. Make sure the curved side is facing up. Carefully remove your instrument.

**STEP 2**    **Statue of Liberty** - Place your left hand on the upper bout and support the bottom of your viola with the right hand. Hold your instrument directly in front of you with the scroll up.

**STEP 3**    **Upside down** - Turn your scroll counterclockwise so the scroll is facing down.

**STEP 4**    **Flat to the ground** - Lift the scroll so the instrument is parallel to the ground at shoulder level.

**STEP 5**    **Bring it in** - Keeping the instrument parallel to the ground, tuck the instrument under your jaw and on top of your collarbone.

**STEP 6**    Identify the strings. Moving from your left to right, the open strings are C (lowest pitch), G, D and A.

**STEP 7**    Pluck each string with your right-hand 1st finger as instructed by your teacher. Plucking is also called *pizzicato* (*pizz.*).

*Statue of Liberty*

*upside down*

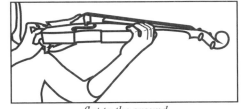

*flat to the ground*

*bring it in*

SB307VLA

SB307TM

2

# PARTS OF THE CELLO AND BOW

## PRACTICE GOOD INSTRUMENT CARE!

### CELLO

1. Always handle your instrument with care and avoid extreme temperatures. It can easily be damaged.

2. Your teacher will show you a safe way to remove the instrument from the case and return it.

3. Wipe the instrument clean with a soft cloth.

4. Always push in your end pin before placing the instrument back in the case.

### BOW

1. Your teacher will show you how to remove the bow, tighten the bow hair and apply rosin.

2. Always loosen the bow hair before putting the bow away.

### SUPPLIES

• rosin
• soft cloth
• end pin rest

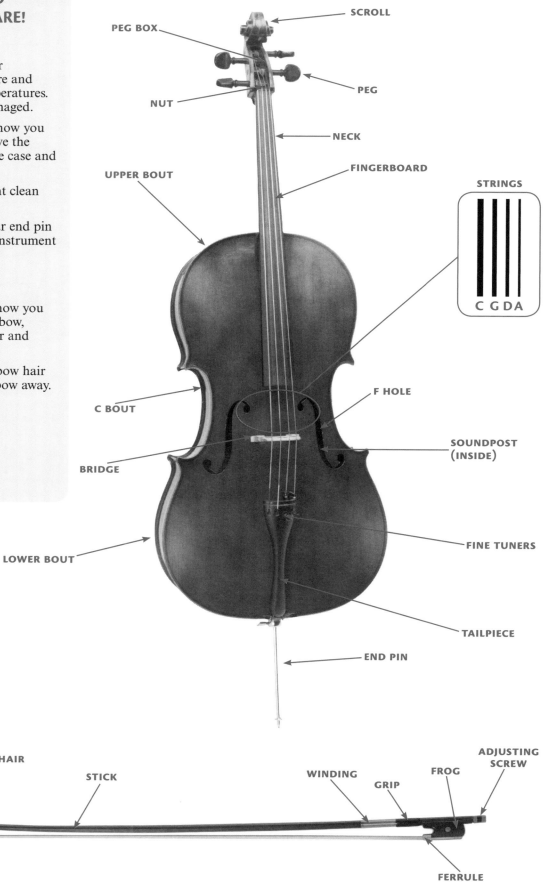

SCROLL

PEG BOX

PEG

NUT

NECK

UPPER BOUT

FINGERBOARD

STRINGS

C G D A

C BOUT

F HOLE

SOUNDPOST (INSIDE)

BRIDGE

LOWER BOUT

FINE TUNERS

TAILPIECE

END PIN

TIP

BOW HAIR

STICK

WINDING

GRIP

FROG

ADJUSTING SCREW

FERRULE

# HOLDING THE INSTRUMENT

**Listen carefully as your teacher explains the proper steps to hold the instrument correctly.**

VIDEO

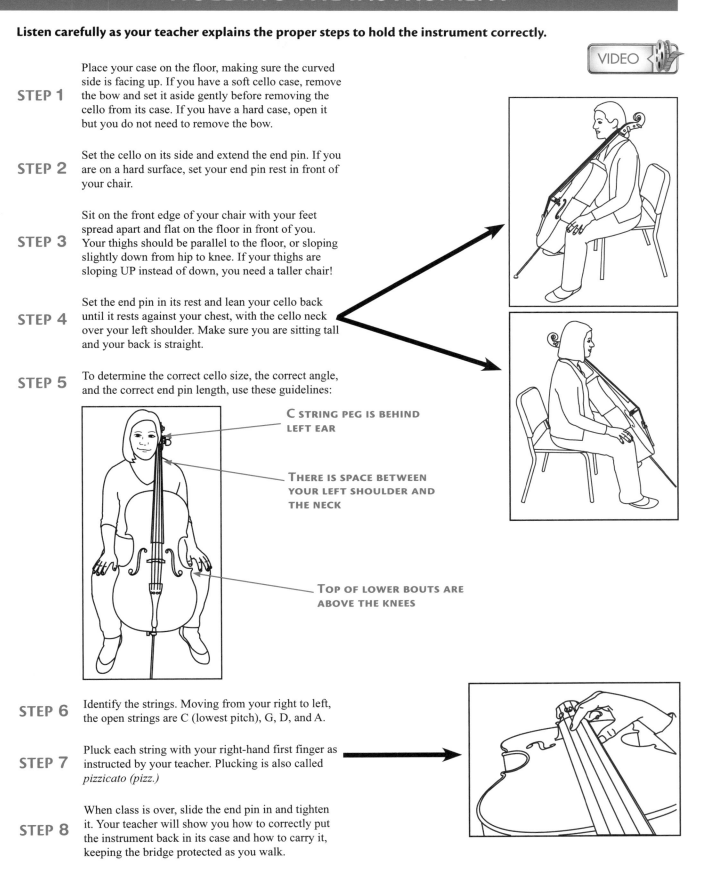

**STEP 1** Place your case on the floor, making sure the curved side is facing up. If you have a soft cello case, remove the bow and set it aside gently before removing the cello from its case. If you have a hard case, open it but you do not need to remove the bow.

**STEP 2** Set the cello on its side and extend the end pin. If you are on a hard surface, set your end pin rest in front of your chair.

**STEP 3** Sit on the front edge of your chair with your feet spread apart and flat on the floor in front of you. Your thighs should be parallel to the floor, or sloping slightly down from hip to knee. If your thighs are sloping UP instead of down, you need a taller chair!

**STEP 4** Set the end pin in its rest and lean your cello back until it rests against your chest, with the cello neck over your left shoulder. Make sure you are sitting tall and your back is straight.

**STEP 5** To determine the correct cello size, the correct angle, and the correct end pin length, use these guidelines:

**C STRING PEG IS BEHIND LEFT EAR**

**THERE IS SPACE BETWEEN YOUR LEFT SHOULDER AND THE NECK**

**TOP OF LOWER BOUTS ARE ABOVE THE KNEES**

**STEP 6** Identify the strings. Moving from your right to left, the open strings are C (lowest pitch), G, D, and A.

**STEP 7** Pluck each string with your right-hand first finger as instructed by your teacher. Plucking is also called *pizzicato (pizz.)*

**STEP 8** When class is over, slide the end pin in and tighten it. Your teacher will show you how to correctly put the instrument back in its case and how to carry it, keeping the bridge protected as you walk.

SB307VC

SB307TM

2

# PARTS OF THE BASS AND BOW

## PRACTICE GOOD INSTRUMENT CARE!

### DOUBLE BASS

1. Always handle your instrument with care and avoid extreme temperatures. It can easily be damaged.

2. Your teacher will show you a safe way to remove the instrument from the case and return it.

3. Wipe the instrument clean with a soft cloth.

4. Always push in your end pin before placing the instrument back in the case.

### BOW

1. Your teacher will show you how to remove the bow, tighten the bow hair and apply rosin.

2. Always loosen the bow hair before putting the bow away.

### SUPPLIES

• rosin
• soft cloth
• end pin rest

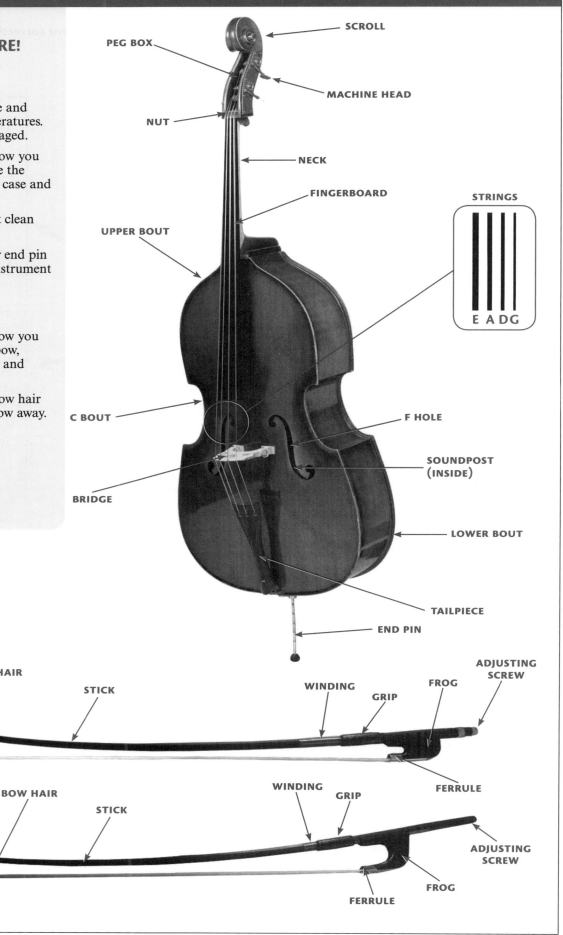

SCROLL

PEG BOX

MACHINE HEAD

NUT

NECK

FINGERBOARD

STRINGS

UPPER BOUT

E A D G

C BOUT

F HOLE

SOUNDPOST (INSIDE)

BRIDGE

LOWER BOUT

TAILPIECE

END PIN

BOW HAIR

STICK

WINDING

GRIP

FROG

ADJUSTING SCREW

TIP

FERRULE

BOW HAIR

STICK

WINDING

GRIP

TIP

ADJUSTING SCREW

FERRULE

FROG

SB307DB

# HOLDING THE INSTRUMENT

**Listen carefully as your teacher explains the proper steps to hold the instrument correctly.**

**STEP 1**  Place your case on the floor, making sure the curved (bridge) side is facing up. Remove the bow from the bow pocket and set it aside gently before removing the bass from its case.

**STEP 2**  Set the bass on its side, extend the endpin and tighten the screw. Stand the bass on its end pin. If you are on a hard surface, you may need to use an end pin rest to keep the bass from slipping on the floor.

**STEP 3**  To measure the correct height of the bass, extend your left arm and place your left hand in the crook of the neck of the bass. Your arm should be straight across. If needed, lay the bass down and adjust your end pin accordingly. Bring the corner of the bass to your stomach.

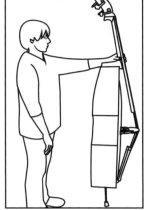

*measuring bass height*    *corner of bass against stomach*

### STANDING

**STEP 4**  If **standing**: Stand tall with your feet spaced about shoulder width. Relax your shoulders and keep your knees flexible (do not lock your knees!). Only the "corner" of the bass should be against your stomach. Since this is the only part of the bass that is in contact with you, the bass will be able to resonate. Balance the bass with the "corner in the stomach" and your left-hand thumb behind the neck of the instrument.

### SITTING

If **sitting**: Sit on the edge of the stool. Place your left foot on the rung of the stool and your right foot on the floor. The "corner" of the bass should be against your stomach and the back of the instrument should rest on the inside of your upper left leg.

**STEP 5**  Identify the strings. Moving from your right to left, the open strings are E (the biggest string and therefore the lowest in pitch) A, D, and G.

**STEP 6**  Pluck each string with your right-hand first finger using the side of your finger instead of the fingertip. Plucking is also call *pizzicato (pizz.)*

**STEP 7**  When class is over, rest your bass on its side, slide the end pin in and tighten the screw. Your teacher will show you how to correctly put the bass back in its case and how to carry it.

SB307DB

SB307TM

# OPUS 1

An **opus** is a number used by composers and publishers who want to organize a group of musical compositions.

**THEORY**

## BEAT

The **beat** is the pulse of the music. A **rhythm** is a pattern that fits within a steady beat.

- Have students practice tapping a steady beat.
- Show examples of an unsteady beat and see if students can identify the difference.

### INTRODUCING THE D STRING | ESTABLISHING PULSE | PIZZICATO

- The open string exercises are useful for establishing a class pulse.
- Be sure the students sing and say the rest out loud from the very first exercise.
- Remind students that when playing pizzicato, the index finger should pull away from the string and not fall onto the fingerboard.
- Have violins / violas sing the note name while celli / basses say rests out loud. Then switch around. Do without instruments and also while playing.

- **Cello tip:** Cellists can keep the left hand resting on the left leg until the left-hand fingers are used starting in 1.10.
- **Bass tip 1:** In addition to regular pizzicato, students can learn a "rest stroke" (classical guitar term) or jazz pizzicato. Use the side of the finger and then have the finger rest on the adjacent lower string after playing the note. The sound will be much louder and there will be fewer blisters on the finger.
- **Bass tip 2:** Remind basses to keep the left hand in the "crook of the neck" until left-hand fingers are used starting in 1.10.

**1.1 BEAT BOX 1** *While plucking your D string, focus on keeping a steady beat!*

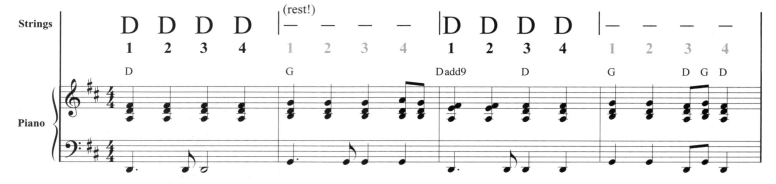

### INTRODUCING THE A STRING

- After learning this exercise, divide the class (e.g. violins/violas on 'team' 1 and celli/basses on 'team' 2) and play 1.1 and 1.2 as a duet!
- **Violin / Viola tip:** As students move to the A string, their right arm should drop slightly. This will help prepare them for changing arm levels with the bow.

- **Cello tip:** As students move to the A string, their right arm should raise slightly. This will help prepare them for changing arm levels with the bow.
- **Bass tip:** Since students are playing an open A string, they should lower their right arm slightly (When bowing, they will raise the arm to play higher strings).

**1.2 BEAT BOX 2** *Practice keeping a steady beat while plucking your A string!*

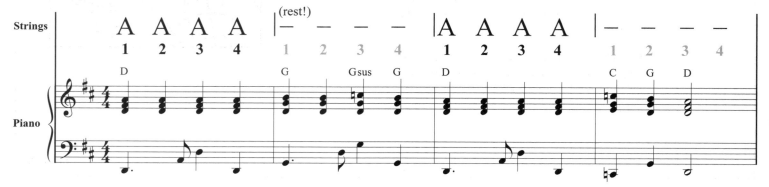

## TRIPLE METER | D AND A STRINGS

- It is not necessary to discuss triple meter at this time, but the teacher may choose to do so. At this stage, students will simply play every note or rest "as it comes." This will prepare students for notated 3/4 time later in the method.
- Without music, slowly practice going from D to A. After students get more comfortable, encourage them to change without looking at strings (this will help them focus on note reading later in the book).
- Clap the exercise, doing something different with the hands on the rests (e.g. hands apart and palms up).

- Have students sing the pitches rather than saying them. This will establish the interval of a fifth (for violin, viola, cello) and fourth (for bass).
- Encourage students to pluck firmly rather than tentatively or overly forceful.
- Students should prepare each new note during a rest.
- **Bass tip:** Point out that basses change strings in a different direction than the other string instruments.

### 1.3 DOUBLE TROUBLE! *Practice playing on your D and A strings!*

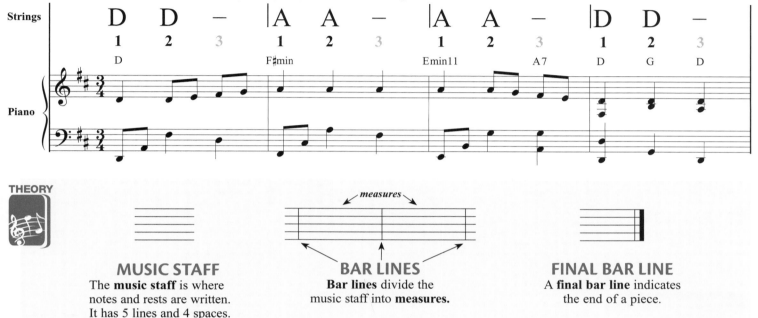

**THEORY**

### MUSIC STAFF
The **music staff** is where notes and rests are written. It has 5 lines and 4 spaces.

*measures*

### BAR LINES
**Bar lines** divide the music staff into **measures.**

### FINAL BAR LINE
A **final bar line** indicates the end of a piece.

- This book intentionally limits the amount of notation introduced at first. Students can focus on posture and playing position. Notation elements are then gradually introduced.

**RHYTHM**

### NOTES AND RESTS
A **quarter note** is one beat of sound.
A **quarter rest** is one beat of silence.

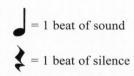

= 1 beat of sound

= 1 beat of silence

## NOTATION FOR D STRING

- Students should sing pitches, then play pizzicato.
- Encourage students to feel the beat during the rests. The accompaniment track will be helpful for this.

- You may choose to model measures 1 and 2 and have students echo you.
- If students are playing in shoulder position, be sure to give frequent rests.

### 1.4 D-LIGHTFUL *Be sure to keep a steady beat, even during the rests!*

SB307TM

- Have students echo you on measure 1. Then isolate measure 3, and finally measure 2.
- Have students clap rhythm before playing.

- Check students' seated position.
- While playing, students may say rests out loud to feel pulse.

**1.5 DARE TO D** *Remember to keep a steady beat for the entire piece!*

**THEORY**

## TREBLE CLEF (VIOLIN)

A **treble clef** names notes on the staff.
The musical alphabet uses A, B, C, D, E, F, and G.

**LINES**

E G B D F

**SPACES**

D F A C E G

## ALTO CLEF (VIOLA)

An **alto clef** names notes on the staff.
The musical alphabet uses A, B, C, D, E, F, and G.

**LINES**

F A C E G

**SPACES**

E G B D F A

## BASS CLEF (CELLO/BASS)

A **bass clef** names notes on the staff.
The musical alphabet uses A, B, C, D, E, F, and G.

**LINES**

G B D F A

**SPACES**

F A C E G B

**THEORY**

# TIME SIGNATURE

The top number shows the number of beats in each measure.
The bottom number shows the type of note that receives one beat.

Number of beats in a measure
Type of note that gets one beat

$\frac{4}{4}$ = 4 ♩    $\frac{3}{4}$ = 3 ♩

- Point out that students have already been playing in both 4/4 and 3/4 time!

---

**NOTATION FOR A STRING | CLEF | TIME SIGNATURE**

- Remind students that they should raise or lower their right arm as they move to the A string (Violins, violas and basses lower; celli raise). Revisit exercise 1.3 if necessary.

- 1.4 and 1.6 can be played as a duet.

## 1.6 A-MAZING

- In preparation, play some echo patterns on D and A. Reinforce height of the right arm.
- Give students frequent rests.
- **Violin / Viola tip:** Check that the instrument is parallel to the floor when in shoulder position.

- **Shoulder position check:** Students should sit on the front half of the chair and keep both feet on the floor. Check frequently to see that no one has the tip or front of the chin in the chin rest (it can be useful to refer to it as the 'jaw' rest). Refer the students to the bottom drawing on page 3 of their book. Model how you yourself do it. Point out that it is the side of your chin (jawbone) that actually rests in the chin rest. Refer again to the last drawing on page 3.

## 1.7 TWO FOR THREE  *Notice how the time signature tells you there are three beats in each measure.*

### THEORY

**REPEAT SIGN**

A **repeat sign** is a final bar line with two dots. Without stopping, go back to the beginning and play the music a second time.

---

INTRODUCING REPEAT SIGN | REINFORCING D AND A STRINGS

- Students should follow the road map by tracking the entire exercise with the fingers before playing.
- Reinforce playing position and posture, drawing attention to arm levels when changing strings.

## 1.8 UPS AND DOWNS

COUNTING | REINFORCING D AND A STRINGS

- Establish that rests are as important as the sounded notes.
- Clap before playing. Students can also sing the exercise (singing is preferred to speaking, as students will naturally improve at sight-singing as they progress through the material).

### **1.9 COUNT REST-ULA** *Count and sing this piece aloud before playing.*

# VIOLIN
## PREPARING THE LEFT HAND

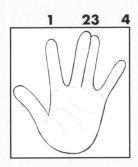

Hold your left hand in front of you, looking at your palm. Space your fingers as shown. Keep this spacing when you move your left hand to the fingerboard.

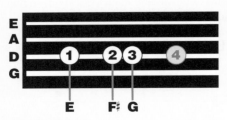

0 – open string
1 – 1st finger
2 – 2nd finger
3 – 3rd finger
4 – 4th finger

## NOTES ON THE D STRING

When you move your left hand to the fingerboard, your teacher will help you be sure that:

- Your thumb is opposite your 1st finger
- Your 1st finger and fingerboard form a square
- There is space underneath the neck of the violin between your thumb and first finger
- The tip of your thumb is pointing toward the ceiling
- Your fingers are curved over the string (creating a "tunnel")
- Your wrist is straight and relaxed

G is played with 3 fingers down

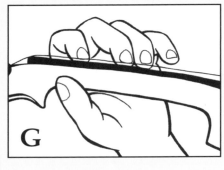

F# is played with 2 fingers down

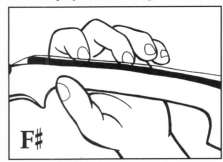

E is played with 1 finger down

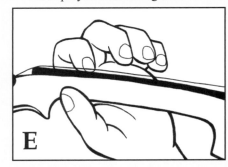

# VIOLA
## PREPARING THE LEFT HAND

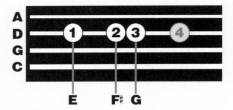

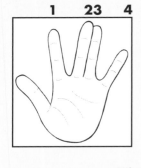

Hold your left hand in front of you, looking at your palm. Space your fingers as shown. Keep this spacing when you move your left hand to the fingerboard.

0 – open string
1 – 1st finger
2 – 2nd finger
3 – 3rd finger
4 – 4th finger

## NOTES ON THE D STRING

When you move your left hand to the fingerboard, your teacher will help you be sure that:

- Your thumb is opposite your 1st finger
- Your 1st finger and fingerboard form a square
- There is space underneath the neck of the viola between your thumb and first finger
- The tip of your thumb is pointing toward the ceiling
- Your fingers are curved over the string (creating a "tunnel")
- Your wrist is straight and relaxed

G is played with 3 fingers down

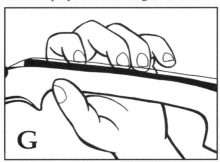

F# is played with 2 fingers down

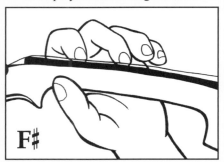

E is played with 1 finger down

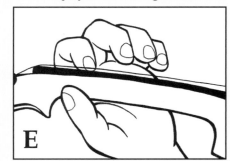

# CELLO

## PREPARING THE LEFT HAND

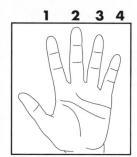

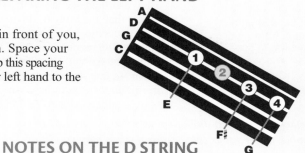

Hold your left hand in front of you, looking at your palm. Space your fingers as shown. Keep this spacing when you move your left hand to the fingerboard.

0 – open string
1 – 1st finger
2 – 2nd finger
3 – 3rd finger
4 – 4th finger

## NOTES ON THE D STRING

When you move your left hand to the fingerboard, your teacher will help you be sure that:

- Your thumb is parallel to the floor and behind your 2nd finger
- Your thumb is touching the center of the back of the neck (be sure it is not squeezing the neck!)

- Your hand makes a "C" shape, as though you are holding a glass of water
- Your fingers are arched over the strings
- Your left elbow is raised just enough so that there is a straight line from the back of your hand to your elbow

G is played with 4 fingers down

F♯ is played with 3 fingers down

E is played with 1 finger down

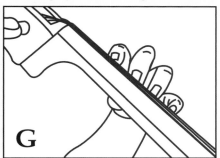

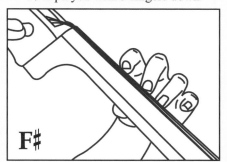

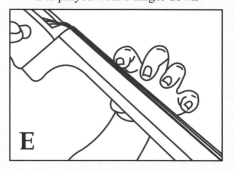

- Watch students carefully to ensure their left hands remain relaxed.
- Give students frequent breaks so they do not develop tension-based habits. Echo work on open strings is a great way to keep them playing while resting the left hand.
- Help students find the correct amount of weight to put on the string (e.g. 10%, 25%, etc.) – source, ASTA Curriculum (2011).
- Students do not need to keep their left hands locked in first position. If violins and violas have good shoulder support, encourage them to move their left hand up and down the fingerboard. Celli and basses can do this easily.

- Whenever you see tension in the left hand, ask students to tap their fingers and thumb. Students can "clap" for themselves with their thumbs. This is a fun way to reduce tension.
- Students who have played piano frequently need reminders about the different fingering system on a stringed instrument. The diagram on page 6 illustrates this.

- Watch to be sure students keep wrists away from the neck.
- **Cello / Bass tip:** The left hand should retain a "C" shape as though holding a glass of water. The thumb should be opposite finger 2.

- **Violin / Viola tip:** Consider setting the finger pattern in guitar position first. They can then see, as well as feel, where the fingers go. If the scroll is held higher than the body of the instrument, it is a short and easy move to the shoulder. Have students model after the left-hand drawing at the top of page 6 just before putting fingers down on the D string. Help students compare the drawing of the finger pattern with straight fingers with the drawing of curved fingers placed down (in that same pattern) on the D String. Some teachers have students move from guitar to shoulder position while holding that finger pattern on the string. If so, students have to pull the elbow in and turn the forearm toward the string.

**1.10 G WHIZ!** **Vln./Vla.** *Remember to keep three fingers down when playing G!*

**Cello** *Remember to keep four fingers down when playing G!*

## BASS
## PREPARING THE LEFT HAND

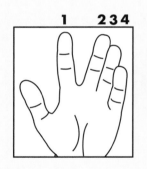

Hold your left hand in front of you, looking at your palm. Space your fingers as shown. Keep this spacing when you move your left hand to the fingerboard.

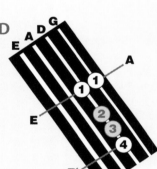

0 – open string
1 – 1st finger
2 – 2nd finger
3 – 3rd finger
4 – 4th finger

## NOTES ON THE D AND G STRINGS

When you move your left hand to the fingerboard, your teacher will help you be sure that:

- Your thumb is parallel to the floor and behind your 2nd finger
- Your thumb is touching the center of the back of the neck (be sure it is not squeezing the neck!)

- Your hand makes a "C" shape, as though you are holding a glass of water
- Your fingers are arched over the strings
- Your left elbow is raised just enough so that there is a straight line from the back of your hand to your elbow

F♯ is played with 4 fingers down on the D string.

E is played with 1 finger down on the D string.

A is played with 1 finger down on the G string.

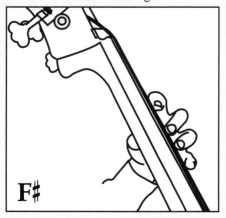

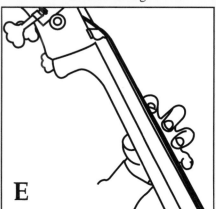

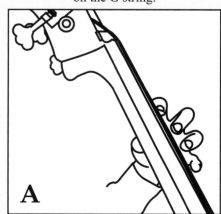

39

**THEORY**

# ACCIDENTALS: SHARP AND NATURAL

**Accidentals** are signs that alter a note's pitch. They are placed to the left of the note.
A **sharp** sign raises the pitch of a note by a half-step. It remains raised for the rest of the measure.
A note without an accidental is called **natural.**

NEW NOTE | INTRODUCTION TO ACCIDENTALS | INTRODUCING THE LEFT HAND (BASS ONLY)

- Fingers should be curved over the string.
- Violins and violas should have both fingers 1 and 2 down. Fingers 3 and 4 should be curved over the string.
- Celli should have fingers 1, 2 and 3 down. Thumb should be parallel to the floor and opposite finger 2.
- Basses will have all four fingers down. The thumb should be behind the neck opposite finger 2.

- **Cello tip:** Finger 4 should hover over the D string. Make sure students do not curl the finger under the fingerboard.
- **Bass tip:** The left arm should be in a straight line from the left wrist. Make sure students do not break the wrist and point the elbow to the floor.
- **Extension:** For teachers who want to get the bow involved early, students can drone a D or A (or both) in quarter or half notes while others play the exercise as written. This is a great way to introduce basic harmony.

### 1.11 SHARP AS A TACK **Vln./Vla.** *Keep both fingers down when playing F♯!*
**Cello** *Keep three fingers down when playing F♯!*
**Bass** *Keep four fingers down when playing F♯!*

- Fingers should always hover over the string, even when they are not being used. When students play F♯, check to make sure that lifted fingers are still curved and hovering close to the string.

- **Bass tip:** Students should prepare F♯ in the first measure to facilitate the transition from G to F♯ in measure 2.

### 1.12 TWO STEP MARCH Vln./Vla. *Keep your fingers over the string, even when they are not being used.*
**Cello** *Keep your 4th finger over the string, even when it is not being used.*
**Bass** *Keep your four fingers hovering over the D string when you play open G.*

- All students use finger 1. Check to make sure fingers 2, 3 and 4 are hovering over the D string.

- **Extension:** Students can use the bow and drone on open A while others play the exercise.

### 1.13 MEET E! *Are your 2nd, 3rd, and 4th fingers over the D string?*

COMBINING G, F♯, AND E

- Have students identify the repeat sign and explain the road map.

- **Bass tip:** Prepare the F♯ on the D string before beginning the exercise. The fingers do not need to be pressed down while playing open G, but they should be ready and hovering.

## 1.14 RUNNING DOWNHILL Bass *Keep all fingers down when playing F♯!*

## D MAJOR TETRACHORD

- You may choose to introduce the word and concept of a tetrachord here. Students love 'advanced' knowledge!

- **Extension:** Students can use the bow and drone on open A while others play the exercise.

## 1.15 DON'T TELL AUNT RHODY!

American Folk Song

- Have students sing and practice the skipped pattern (D to F#) before introducing notation. When putting down two or more fingers, students should make sure that all fingers land on the string simultaneously.

- **Extension:** Students can use the bow and drone on open A while others play the exercise.

## 1.16 AU CLAIRE DE LA LUNE

French Folk Song

**Vln./Vla.** *Notice the skip in measure 3. Put down your 1st and 2nd fingers at the same time.*
**Cello** *Notice the skip in measure 3. Put down fingers 1, 2, and 3 at the same time.*
**Bass** *Notice the skip in measure 3. Put down all four fingers at the same time.*

- In addition to the tunnel, check to see that students are keeping their wrist away from the neck. In order to get a clear sound on the D string, the fingers have to be curved and not touch the A string at all.
- **Violin / Viola tip:** The left elbow seldom just hangs down directly under the middle of the instrument. They must "pull" it a little bit to the right of the middle, pointing to the bellybutton, and rotate the wrist a little bit to the left to put the fingers into the right position to tunnel over the A string. Make frequent reminders that curved fingers and a straight wrist are important, and that both are necessary to make the "tunnel" work. It is a good idea to point out the drawing on page 7 that illustrates this rotation of the wrist that makes the tunnel possible. It may take many tries before some are able to master this.

- **Extension:** After you ensure students understand the concept of the tunnel, you may choose introduce 4th finger to violinists and violists. Motivated cellists could be introduced to 2nd position for the first two measures (2nd position is further explained on page 24 of the student book).

**Violin**

**Viola**

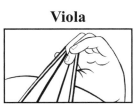

**Cello**

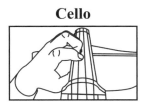

**Bass New Note: A**

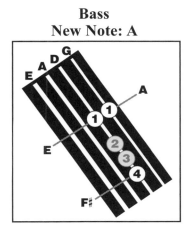

## 1.17 TUNNELING THROUGH

**Vln./Vla./Cello** *When you see a bracket, keep your fingers down. The A string should tunnel under your fingers. If your A rings clearly while your fingers stay on the D string, you have a clear tunnel!*
**Bass** *When changing from E to A, your first finger should lift completely off the D string and "hop" over to the G string.*

**HISTORY**

### MUSIC

**Ludwig van Beethoven** (1770–1827) was a German composer and pianist. He began to suffer hearing loss at an early age, and by the time his Ninth Symphony and its *Ode to Joy* were performed, he was completely deaf!

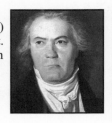

### SCIENCE

The same year Beethoven finished his Ninth Symphony, William Buckland wrote the first ever account of fossil bones that had come from a giant reptile. He named it "Megalosaurus" (great lizard), which would later become known as a dinosaur.

### WORLD

Also in 1824, Louis Braille had largely completed a new 6-dot system to help the blind and visually impaired read and write. Braille was only 15 years old at the time!

- Draw connections between Beethoven and what was happening in science and world history at the same time. This will help students understand the time period and world in which Beethoven was writing.

- Listen to recordings of some other Beethoven works. Ask students to compare and contrast them with *Ode to Joy.*

**REINFORCING TUNNEL SHAPE | STRING CROSSING | BEETHOVEN**

- You may choose to introduce (by rote) the traditional rhythm in measures 4 and 8.
- This is the first exercise that takes up two lines. Have students use their fingers to track the entire piece (skipping to the second line) before playing.

- **Extension:** Have a discussion about the premiere of the piece and what it may have been like for Beethoven who was deaf at the time.

**1.18 ODE TO JOY** **Vln./Vla./Cello** *Keep your fingers down when you see a bracket and strive for a clear tunnel!*
**Bass** *Keep all fingers down when playing F♯!*

Ludwig van Beethoven

*continue to the next line*

## VIOLA/CELLO/BASS
## LEDGER LINES

**Ledger lines** extend the staff.
Notes written above or below the
staff appear with ledger lines.

- Ledger lines are introduced for viola, cello and bass at this time.
  Violinists will see this information on page 25 of the student book (Teacher's Manual page 118).

## VIOLIN
### NOTES ON THE A STRING

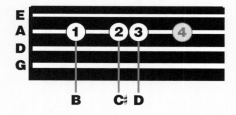

D is played with 3 fingers down | C♯ is played with 2 fingers down | B is played with 1 finger down

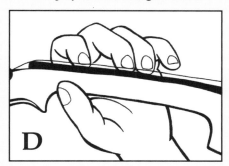
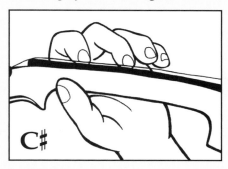
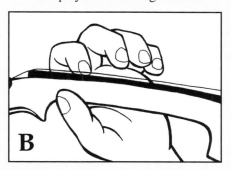

## VIOLA
### NOTES ON THE A STRING

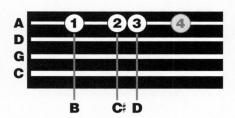

D is played with 3 fingers down | C♯ is played with 2 fingers down | B is played with 1 finger down

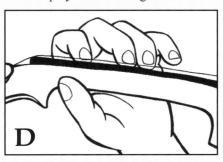
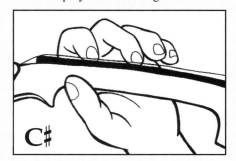
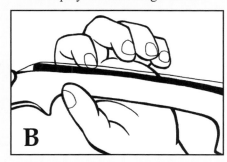

SB307TM

# CELLO
## NOTES ON THE A STRING

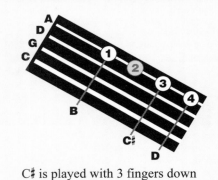

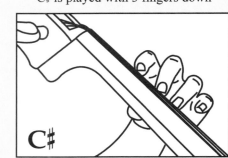

D is played with 4 fingers down

C♯ is played with 3 fingers down

B is played with 1 finger down

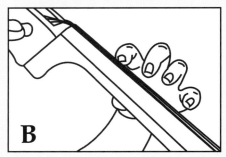

**SHIFTING**

# BASS
## THIRD (III) POSITION ON THE G STRING

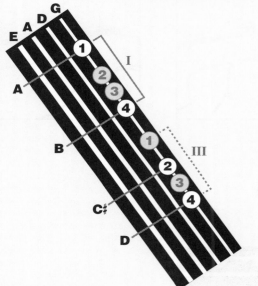

Up until now, you have been playing in first (I) position. To play in **third (III) position**, shift your left hand toward the bridge (the pitch will go up) so that your 4th finger D is in tune with your open D. Your thumb should also move, staying relaxed and behind your 2nd finger.

Roman numerals (I and III) are used to indicate when you shift positions. In addition, a dash is always put in front of the first fingering in a new position. In this book, you will also see a dotted bracket above sections that shift into different positions.

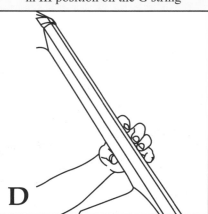

D is played with 4 fingers down in III position on the G string

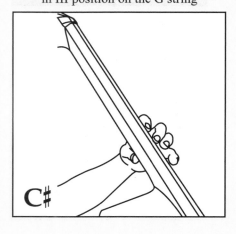

C♯ is played with 2 fingers down in III position on the G string

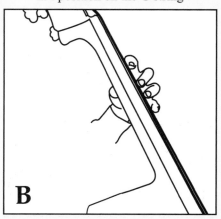

B is played with 4 fingers down in I position on the G string

- **Bass tip:** Dotted brackets are used for the first half of the book to highlight when students shift to III position. They are removed in Opus 3.

**NEW NOTE: D | III POSITION (BASS ONLY)**

- Violins, violas and celli should imagine a straight line between the elbow, wrist and hand. The hand is slightly closed compared to the position on the D string.
- When violins, violas and cellos compare this exercise with 1.10, they should notice that it uses the same rhythm and same fingering, just on a different string!

- **Bass tip:** It is helpful if basses have the D and C♯ in III position marked on the fingerboard. Encourage students to hear how high D should be in tune with open D. Reiterate that the thumb should stay relaxed and behind finger 2.

**1.19 SAILING THE HIGH Ds** Vln./Vla./Cello *Compare this line to 1.10 G Whiz! Do you notice any similarities?*
**Bass** *A dotted bracket indicates to stay in the notated position.*

**NEW NOTE: C♯ | REINFORCING III POSITION (BASS ONLY)**

- Encourage students to avoid writing in additional note names or fingerings. Note names and fingerings have been strategically placed to create a successful music reading experience.

**1.20 DOWN AND UP** Bass *When shifting, remember to keep your thumb and 2nd finger opposite each other.*

SB307TM

- **Extension:** Explain the eight notes of an octave include the starting and ending note. Ask students what songs have an octave in them (e.g. *Somewhere Over the Rainbow, Take Me Out to the Ball Game*).

**1.21 HIGH OCTANE** Vln./Vla./Cello *Keep your fingers down on the A string when you see a bracket. Listen for a clear, ringing D string!*
**Bass** *Keep your fingers down on the G string while playing open D.*

**Additional bass specific exercises are included throughout the method book.**
**They always include a letter in the title (e.g. 1.21a) and are designated for basses only.**

## NEW NOTE (BASS ONLY)

- **Extension:** Remind bassists to keep all four fingers down while playing 4th finger.

### 1.21a MEET B! - Basses Only

PRACTICE SHIFTING INTO AND OUT OF III POSITION ON THE G STRING

## 1.21b III... TO... I... LIFT OFF! - Basses Only *Your fingers should stay in light contact with the G string when shifting to and from III position.*

PRACTICE SHIFTING INTO AND OUT OF III POSITION ON THE G STRING

- Remind students that the fingers should stay in light contact with the string while shifting to and from III position. The thumb should stay relaxed and behind finger 2.

- This exercise is ideal to prepare 1.22 *Cold Cross Buns.*

## 1.21c PREPARING COLD BUNS - Basses Only

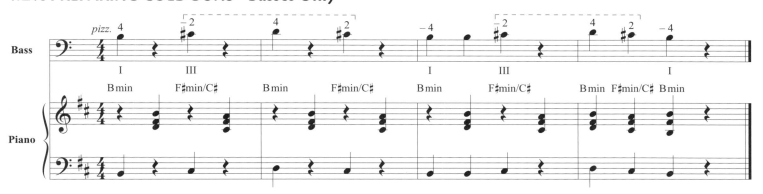

NEW NOTE: B

- **Extension:** Discuss why the piece is called *Cold Cross Buns* instead of *Hot Cross Buns.*
  Play the piece for them in major instead of minor (using D♯ instead of D natural).

## 1.22 COLD CROSS BUNS

English Folk Melody

- Have students sing the interval and practice playing the Major 3rd before introducing the notation.
- **Cello tip:** Be sure that finger 4 is hovering over the A string.

- **Bass tip:** Basses are required to do a lot of shifting in this piece. Directors may choose to have them play 1.23a *Groovin' Grandpa* instead, which allows ample time between each shift. This can be played along with 1.23 *Groovin' Grandma*.

## 1.23 GROOVIN' GRANDMA

Traditional American Melody

## 1.23a GROOVIN' GRANDPA - Basses Only *Play this along with or instead of 1.23 Groovin' Grandma.*

- Forming the bow hold on a pencil, straw or dowel rod will help students learn the correct bow hold and make the transfer to the actual bow easier.

- Students should practice this workout daily.
- Additional resource: *The ASTA String Curriculum. Right Hand Skills and Knowledge: Baseline Skills.*

## VIOLIN/VIOLA
## BOW WORKOUT NO. 1: PREPARING THE RIGHT HAND

Using a pencil, do the following:

1. **FLOP** - Hold the pencil in your left hand, parallel to the floor. **Flop** your right-hand fingers on the pencil.

2. **PARK AND CURVE** - **Park** the pinky on the pencil. Make sure it is **curved**.

3. **SMILE** - Place your thumb behind the tallest finger. Your thumb nail should rest against the pencil and the thumb joint is curved like a **smile**.

4. **STIR** - Rotate your pencil to the right so it is vertical. Check your thumb to be sure it is still curved. Flex fingers and thumb as though you are **stirring** a small cup of soup. Your fingers should be slightly tilted as in the illustration.

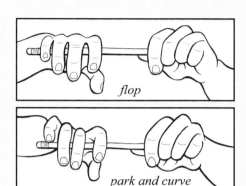

*flop*

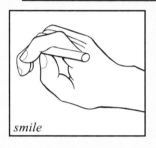

*park and curve*

*smile*

*stir*

## CELLO
## BOW WORKOUT NO. 1: PREPARING THE RIGHT HAND

Using a pencil, do the following:

1. **FLOP** - Hold the pencil in your left hand, parallel to the floor. **Flop** your right-hand fingers on the pencil.

2. **SEPARATE AND REST** - Gently **separate** your fingers and let your pinky **rest** against the pencil.

3. **SMILE** - Place your thumb behind the tallest finger. Your thumb nail should rest against the pencil and the thumb joint is curved like a **smile**.

4. **STIR** - Rotate your pencil to the right so it is vertical. Check your thumb to be sure it is still curved. Flex fingers and thumb as though you are **stirring** a cup of soup.

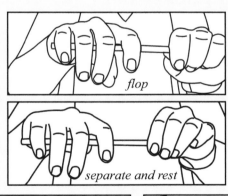

*flop*

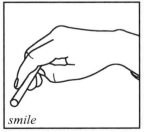

*separate and rest*

*smile*

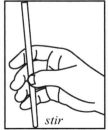

*stir*

# BASS

## BOW WORKOUT NO. 1: PREPARING THE RIGHT HAND

There are two different types of bass bows, each with its own bow hold.
Your teacher will help you choose which one is best for you.

### FRENCH BOW HOLD

Using a pencil, do the following:

**1 FLOP** - Hold the pencil in your left hand, parallel to the floor.
**Flop** your right-hand fingers on the pencil.

**2 SEPARATE AND REST** - Gently **separate** your fingers and let
your pinky **rest** against the pencil.

**3 SMILE** - Place your thumb behind the tallest finger. Your thumb
nail should rest against the pencil and the thumb joint is curved
like a **smile**.

**4 STIR** - Rotate your pencil to the right so it is vertical. Check your
thumb to be sure it is still curved. Flex fingers and thumb as though
you are **stirring** a cup of soup.

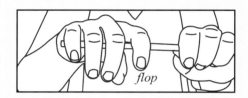

*flop*

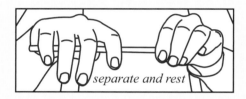

*separate and rest*

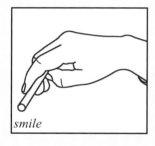

*smile*

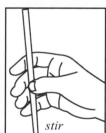

*stir*

### GERMAN BOW HOLD

Using a pencil, do the following:

**1** Hold the pencil in your left hand, parallel to the floor.
Shake and relax your right hand.

**2** Touch the palm of your hand with the pencil.

**3** Bring the tips of your thumb, first, and second fingers together on
the pencil. Keep your hand relaxed.

**4** Flex your fingers and thumb.

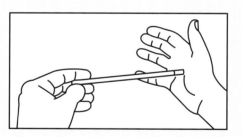

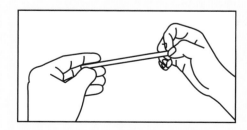

DESCENDING D MAJOR SCALE

- Isolate measures 2 and 3 so students can practice crossing the string and preparing their fingers accordingly.

## 1.24 D MAJOR MARCH

ASCENDING D MAJOR SCALE

- Isolate measures 2 and 3 so students can practice crossing the string and preparing their fingers accordingly.

- **Extension:** Students can play line 1.24 and 1.25 together as a duet.

## 1.25 ON THE WAY UP

- Encourage students to keep fingers down on the D string as they play the A in measure 4.

- Students can prepare the first note of the piece by playing D, E and then F♯. This way the first note will be in tune.

### 1.26 MARY HAD A LITTLE LAMB Bass *Practice measure 4 alone, moving only your 1st finger to play A while your other fingers hover over the D string.*

Traditional

MAINTAINING LEFT HAND POSITION

- Continue to reinforce that fingers should remain down where indicated with a solid bracket. Listen for a clear, ringing D string.

**1.27 TRAMPOLINE!** Bass *Keep fingers down where indicated with a solid bracket.*

The following studies are provided in the bass book to reinforce shifting between first and third position.
Remind basses to keep fingers in contact with the string while shifting.

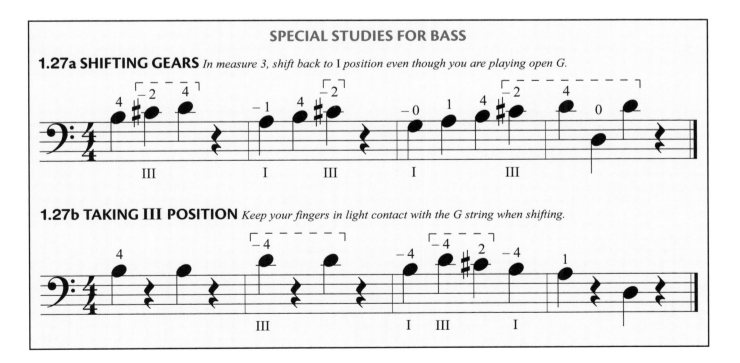

As with Bow Workout No. 1, students should practice this workout daily.

# VIOLIN/VIOLA
## BOW WORKOUT NO. 2: MOVING FROM THE ELBOW

1 Follow the steps in Bow Workout No. 1 (flop, park and curve, smile, stir).

2 Keep your bow hand relaxed and your thumb curved. Make sure your fingers are tilted slightly.

3 **Point** your left index finger at the crease of your right elbow.

4 **Open and close** the hinge of your elbow. Keep your right shoulder as still and relaxed as possible.

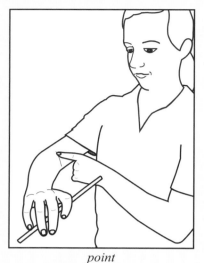
*point*

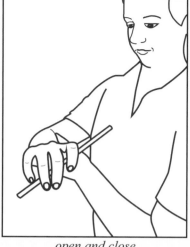
*open and close*

# CELLO
## BOW WORKOUT NO. 2: MOVING FROM THE ELBOW

1 Follow the steps in Bow Workout No.1 (flop, separate and rest, smile, stir).

2 Keep your bow hand relaxed and your thumb curved.

3 **Open and close** the hinge of your elbow slightly. At the same time, **swing** your elbow away from and back toward your body.

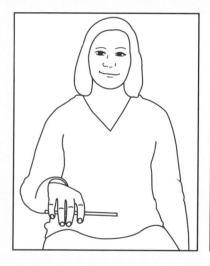

*open and close, swing*

# BASS
## BOW WORKOUT NO. 2: MOVING FROM THE ELBOW

1 Follow the steps in Bow Workout No. 1.

2 Keep your bow hand relaxed and your thumb curved.

3 **Open and close** the hinge of your elbow slightly. At the same time, **swing** your elbow away from and back toward your body.

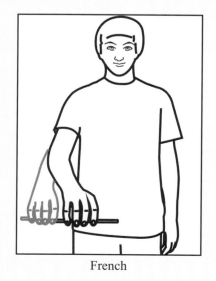
French

German

ASCENDING AND DESCENDING D MAJOR SCALE

- Encourage students to use the rests to look ahead and prepare for the following measure, especially when crossing strings.

## 1.28 BREAKING IT DOWN

# MAJOR SCALE

A **major scale** has eight notes going up or down in consecutive order. Your D Major Scale includes all the notes you have learned in Opus 1. Notice that the top and bottom notes of the scale are both D.

## DEVELOPING TECHNIQUE WITH THE D MAJOR SCALE

- If students struggle with the descending pattern in the last four measures (crossing strings without a rest), have them play only on beats 1 and 3 until they are more comfortable. Then play as written.

- **Bass tip:** Remind students to keep all fingers on the string while playing finger 4.

## 1.29 D MAJOR SCALE

# OPUS 1 ENCORE

## INTERPRETATION STATION

*Interpretation Station* focuses on students' ability to listen to and make judgments about performance, style, expression, and contrasts.

- In this assessment, we focus on music and its ability to communicate emotion. While designed as part of a unit assessment, this particular assessment can be used anytime (even before students have instruments).

- Students should listen to the example in class or at home and write a journal entry describing the music.
- Encourage students to use vocabulary they have learned in Opus 1.

Listen to the corresponding track on the DVD. Describe the music and how it makes you feel. Why does it make you feel that way?

**Music:** *Heart of Fire* by Lauren Bernofsky

- After the students have listened to the music and recorded their thoughts, ask them if the title fits the music.

## SIMON SEZ

*Simon "Sez"* is an assessment of the development of aural skills. Performance skills gained from reading are discrete and different from performance skills guided by aural cues.

Below is a transcription of the melody students hear on the DVD. Students, however, do not have anything in their books.

- Students may complete this particular assessment any time after line 1.17.
- Teachers may choose to supplement with their own echo patterns that are better tailored for the ability of their students.

- Have students critique themselves and each other. Did they match the recording?

Listen to the corresponding track on the DVD. You will hear a series of four-note patterns. Listen to the patterns and echo them back. *Hint: the first pattern starts on your open D string!*

## COMPOSER'S CORNER

*Composer's Corner* allows you to assess students' ability to transfer skills acquired from exercises specific to each Opus into a created product. It is a synthesis exercise to help you assess higher order thinking.

- Students may complete this particular assessment any time after line 1.12.

- Consider repeating the assessment as the students learn new notes.

A composer is someone who creates original music. It is your turn to be a composer! Begin by adding the alto clef, bass clef, treble clef, time signature, and final barline in the music. Then you can complete the piece using notes you already know. Guide rhythms have been provided for you.

Add these symbols to your piece!

## PENCIL POWER

*Pencil Power* assessments allow you to assess students' ability to identify certain musical concepts generally found in the written score. It also assesses broader musical knowledge.

- Students may complete this particular assessment any time after line 1.23.

Review the following notes. Write in each note name below and add the fingering above.

## CURTAIN UP!

The *Curtain Up!* section includes a performance piece covering material that has been reviewed in Opus 1. Students should be encouraged to use the DVD and give full performances for friends and family. This is also a time to learn performance and concert etiquette. Students should introduce each piece by title and acknowledge applause by bowing.

Time to perform! The following music showcases what you have learned in Opus 1.

ASSESSMENT OF ALL SKILLS PRESENTED IN OPUS 1

- Teachers should look for the following elements:
  1. Proper playing position
  2. Fingers are curved
  3. Wrist is straight
  4. Student is keeping fingers down where indicated with brackets
  5. Student is striving for a resonant pizzicato sound

**1.30 STROLLIN' IN THE SAND** Vln./Vla./Cello *Remember to keep your fingers down when possible.*

## BOW-NUS!

The *Bow-Nus!* section focuses on bow technique. Students may practice this particular assessment any time after Bow Workout No. 2 on page 10 of the student book.

Demonstrate a great bow hold with a pencil. Open and close your elbow to the following rhythm.

**1.31 EL-BOW!**

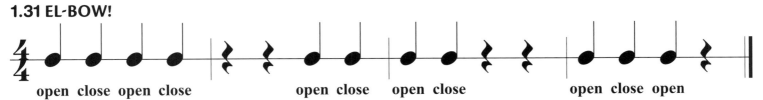

SB307TM

# OPUS 2

**Students should only move to the bow after they have mastered Bow Workout No. 1 and 2. Once the bow hold is set, they can move immediately into Bow Workout No. 4 and the Bow Beat Exercises.**

## VIOLIN/VIOLA

### BOW WORKOUT NO. 3: BOW HOLD

1. Begin by using the early bow hold (your hand will be at the balance point of the bow).

2. Your teacher will show you how much to tighten the bow by turning the adjusting screw clockwise.

3. Hold the bow with both hands making sure the bow hair is facing the floor and the frog of the bow is to your right.

4. While supporting the bow in your left hand, form a good bow hold with your right hand. Remember: *flop, park and curve, smile!*

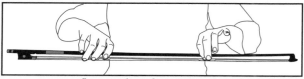
*flop, park and curve, smile!*

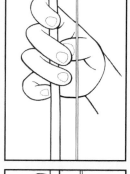

5. Point the tip of the bow in the air with only your right hand. Flex your fingers (*stir!*).

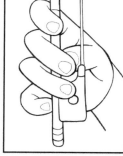

6. Your teacher will determine the ideal time for you to move to a regular bow hold.

## CELLO

### BOW WORKOUT NO. 3: BOW HOLD

1. Begin by using the early bow hold (your hand will be at the balance point of the bow).

2. Your teacher will show you how much to tighten the bow by turning the adjusting screw clockwise.

3. Hold the bow with both hands making sure the bow hair is facing the floor and the frog of the bow is to your right.

4. While supporting the bow in your left hand, form a good bow hold with your right hand. Remember: *flop, separate and rest, smile!*

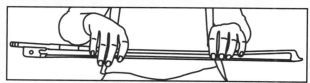
*flop, separate and rest, smile!*

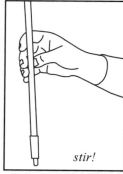
*stir!*

5. Point the tip of the bow in the air with only your right hand. Flex your fingers (*stir!*).

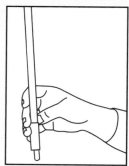

6. Your teacher will determine the ideal time for you to move to a regular bow hold.

# BASS
## BOW WORKOUT NO. 3: BOW HOLD

**1** If you are using a French bow, begin by using the early bow hold (your hand will be at the balance point of the bow.)

**2** Your teacher will show you how much to tighten the bow by turning the adjusting screw clockwise.

**3** Hold the bow with both hands making sure the bow hair is facing the floor and the frog of the bow is to your right.

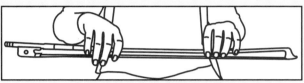

*flop, separate and rest, smile!*

**4a** While supporting the bow in your left hand, form a good bow hold with your right hand. Remember the following for the French bow hold: flop, separate and rest, smile!

For the German bow:

**4b**
    a. Put the tips of your thumb, first, and second fingers together.
    b. Open them just enough to place the bow in your right hand so that the frog touches your palm.
    c. Bring your fingers back together on the bow
    d. Place your pinky under the bow so it is touching the ferrule.

French Bow Hold
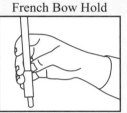

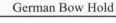
German Bow Hold
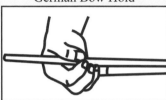

# NOTE TO THE TEACHER: AN ALTERNATIVE METHOD OF SETTING THE BOW HOLD FOR VIOLIN AND VIOLA (THE "INSIDE" LOOK)

**1** The teacher models and the students copy an open right hand, palm up, as if it were going to catch a medium size orange, which you will pretend to toss to each student.

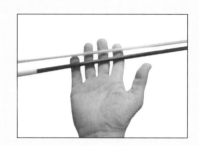

**2** Pick up the bow with the left hand at the frog, upside down. Students can hold the frog any way they want – most will probably clasp it within a fist-like hold, but it does not matter. Model this step too, and they will probably copy what you do.

**3** With the bow horizontal, but in front of them upside down, slide the right hand fingers to the underside of the stick (still palm up) starting at the tip (or frog, if teacher prefers). Students should slide their hands up across the stick until they locate the balance point, using only the left hand to gently stabilize it.

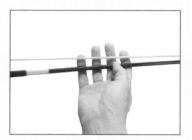

**4** Tell the students to look at their thumbs and then bend them inward toward the stick. Move the thumb (still bent) toward the 2nd finger until the tip meets the stick opposite that 2nd finger. Model and remind them that the tip of the thumb contacts the stick at the thumbnail.

**5** Curl the three long fingers just a little to help maintain the balance, but do not let students squeeze their thumbs to help with balance. Thumb tension is the enemy! Model and explain where the pinkie goes; again on its tip, not the pad for upper strings.

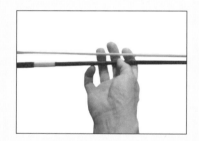

**6** After a final visual check, rotate the bow until the fingers are on top. With violins on laps, repeat, and when the left hand is free, place the instrument in playing position. Demonstrate and practice some "helicopter" landings from directly above on the middle strings, keeping the right arm level (on an even plane) when the bow is on the D string.

**7** After a brief rest for the students (while you demonstrate the whole activity again), get the students to set their bow holds this way again and helicopter land the hairs on the string midway between bridge and fingerboard just a little further up the string from their right hand 1st fingers. If they look good and appear ready, begin some easy open string echo exercises, with frequent reminders to open the elbow on the first note and keep thumbs curved. You should soon be ready to play the exercises on page 13 of the student book.

**8** The trickiest part of this, or any first arco playing, will probably be picking up and setting the violin in playing position without help from the right hand. Cellists and bassists have a slight advantage at this stage because their instrument is supported between body and floor.

# VIOLIN/VIOLA
## BOW WORKOUT NO. 4: ROSIN BOWING

1  Using your left hand, hold your rosin near your left shoulder with the rosin cake facing away from you.

2  Place the bow on the rosin.

3  Moving from the elbow (like you did when you pointed at the crease), practice moving the bow up and down.

4  Remember to keep your right shoulder as still and relaxed as possible. Open and close from the hinge of your elbow.

# CELLO
## BOW WORKOUT NO. 4: ROSIN BOWING

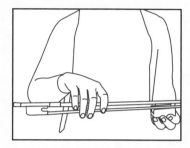

1  Using your left hand, hold your rosin in front of you at waist level and parallel to the floor.

2  Place the bow on the rosin.

3  Open and close the hinge of your elbow slightly. At the same time, swing your elbow away from and back toward your body.

4  Remember to keep your right shoulder as still and relaxed as possible.

# BASS
## BOW WORKOUT NO. 4: ROSIN AND TUBE BOWING

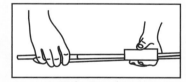

1  Using your left hand, hold your rosin in front of you at waist level and parallel to the floor.

2  Place the bow on the rosin near the frog.

3  Open the hinge of your elbow slightly. At the same time, swing your elbow away from your body. When you run out of bow, lift it, move back to the frog, and start again. You can also use a tube to practice bowing in both directions.

4  Remember to keep your right shoulder as still and relaxed as possible.

Tube Bowing

- Bow Workouts 3 and 4 are extensions of the previous Bow Workouts. It may be helpful to review Bow Workout No. 2 just before taking out the bow. It will help establish muscle memory (especially if students have been practicing the workouts since they were first introduced).

- **Violin / Viola tip:** Be sure students form a square between the clavicle, lower right arm, lower left arm and the bow. Students should move from the elbow, with minimal movement in the shoulder.

- **Cello tip:** To maintain a stable bow hold, students may benefit from using a lighter bow from a smaller sized instrument. Cellists and bassists do not have the "counter-balance" of their fourth finger on the stick (as violinists/violists do). As the bow hold becomes more secure, move back to the proper size bow.

- **Bass tip 1:** When working on the bow hold without the bass, the student should hold the bow with two hands (the left hand helping with the weight of the bow). When they transfer the bow to the instrument, the weight of the bow will be held by the strings.

- **Bass tip 2:** Since bass rosin is very sticky, bass players are not able to do an up bow on rosin. A tube is an effective way of getting students to practice bowing in both directions. Down bows on rosin are excellent practice both for bowing and also for teaching students to rosin their bows.

 = **down bow**  A down bow symbol looks like the frog of the bow. Lead with the frog and open from the elbow.

V = **up bow**  An up bow symbol looks like the tip of the bow. Lead with the tip and close from the elbow.

SB307TM

- Violinists and violists should hold rosin at the left shoulder to promote moving from the right elbow, not the right shoulder.
- Point out the text that appears under the rests in measures 2 and 4.

- Observe that cellists and bassists are swinging and unfolding their arms properly.
- Have the students begin with the middle third of the bow.

### 2.1 BOW BEAT No. 1 Vln./Vla. *Rosin bow, making sure you are moving from the elbow, not the shoulder.*
**Cello/Bass** *Rosin (tube) bow, making sure you are swinging from the elbow.*

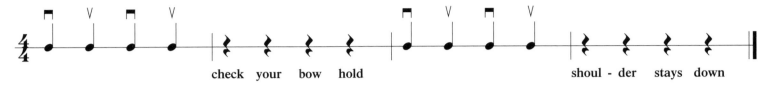

check your bow hold          shoul - der stays down

ROSIN BOWING | TUBE BOWING (BASS ONLY)

- Encourage students to keep the bow still during rests
- **ERRATA:** On early versions of the cello book, line 2.2 is printed incorrectly. Teachers can either project the correct line or download a corrected page at www.fjhmusic.com.

- Bass players are instructed to tube bow instead of rosin bow.

### 2.2 BOW BEAT No. 2 *Rosin (tube) bow. Is your right shoulder still and relaxed while you are bowing?*

1  2  3  1  2  3  1  2  3  1  2  3

## PLACING THE BOW ON THE STRING

- Students will need a healthy amount of practice using the bow on the string before reading out of the book and bowing at the same time.
- Echo exercises are ideal at this point in student development
- Circulate throughout the class, helping students draw a straight bow. The bow should be at a right angle with the string for the best possible tone.

- Watch for excess shoulder movement, particularly in violin and viola
- **Cello tip:** If the tip of the bow begins to point toward the floor, the bow is too heavy for the student. If a smaller/lighter bow is not accessible, consider moving the grip closer to the balance point. Make sure the thumb is curved.
- **Bass tip:** Unlike the rest of the students, have bassists use just the lower half of the bow for a great sound.

## VIOLIN/VIOLA
## FROM ROSIN TO STRING!

VIDEO

1 Place the bow on your D string between the end of the fingerboard and the bridge.

2 Your bow should be parallel to the bridge. Keep your right shoulder down and relaxed.

*early bow hold*

*regular bow hold*

# CELLO
## FROM ROSIN TO STRING!

*early bow hold*

*regular bow hold*

**1** Place the bow on your D string between the end of the fingerboard and the bridge.

**2** Your bow should be parallel to the bridge. Keep your right shoulder down and relaxed.

# BASS
## FROM ROSIN AND TUBE TO STRING!

*French bow hold*

*German bow hold*

**1** Place the bow on your D string between the end of the fingerboard and the bridge.

**2** Your bow should be parallel to the bridge. Keep your right shoulder down and relaxed.

## BOWING ON THE D STRING

- Consider making straw 'bridges' (insert straws between the upper part of the f holes) to help them draw a straight bow.

- Point out the text that appears under the rests in measures 2 and 4.

**2.3 BEST IN BOW** *Use an award-winning bow hold and keep the bow parallel to the bridge!*

- Ask the students to identify this same rhythmic pattern on page 12.

- Students can practice this saying "rest" aloud *and* internally so they keep a steady pulse throughout.

### 2.4 ON THE HORIZON *Notice that the time signature tells you there are three beats in each measure.*

BOWING ON THE A STRING | ARM LEVEL CHANGE

- Reinforce arm levels before playing the exercise.
- Bows should remain parallel to the bridge and perpendicular to the string.

- **Cello tip:** The change to the A string can cause the bow tip to move toward the floor and the bow hold to collapse.

### 2.5 A NEW ANGLE *Make sure you are moving from the elbow, not the shoulder.*

BOWING ON THE A STRING | 3/4 TIME

- Students should continue to keep right shoulder relaxed.
- Have students compare this rhythm with line 2.4.

- **Extension:** This can lead into discussion of a waltz. If students are seated, have them tap their toes to the beat – one left-foot tap followed by two right-foot taps.

## 2.6 WALTZ OF THE BOWS

 **VIOLIN**
### ARM LEVELS

The level of your arm changes when you bow different strings.

Move your **arm down** to play **higher strings.**
Move your **arm up** to play **lower strings.**

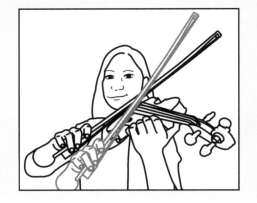

 **VIOLA**
### ARM LEVELS

The level of your arm changes when you bow different strings.

Move your **arm down** to play **higher strings.**
Move your **arm up** to play **lower strings.**

 **CELLO**
### ARM LEVELS

The level of your arm changes when you bow different strings.

Move your **arm up** to play **higher strings.**
Move your **arm down** to play **lower strings.**

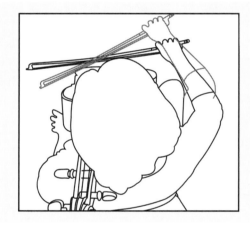

 **BASS**
### ARM LEVELS

The level of your arm changes when you bow different strings.

Move your **arm up** to play **higher strings.**
Move your **arm down** to play **lower strings.**

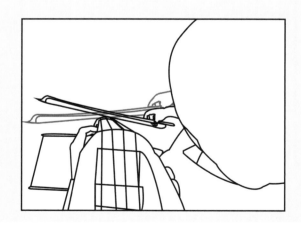

- Students should do some rote practice changing strings before reading notated music.
- Students can feel the nuance of changing from D to A more easily if they first go from their lowest string to their highest string (so students can experience extreme movement of the arm first, then the more nuanced movement between D and A). Have violins and basses move from G to E. Violas and celli will move from C to A.

- Consider doing various echo patterns and end with a pattern that is the same as line 2.7. They will be well prepared and successful as a result!

## CHANGING ARM LEVELS WHEN CHANGING STRINGS

- The bow should remain perpendicular to the strings.
- Point out the text below the rests and encourage students to internalize the words as they play.

## 2.7 CROSS TRAINING

## REINFORCING ARM LEVELS | 3/4 TIME

- Remind students to only move the bow angle as much as needed.
- Isolate measures 3 and 4 so students can practice changing string levels without rests.

## 2.8 SWITCH HITTER *Your up bows should sound the same as your down bows!*

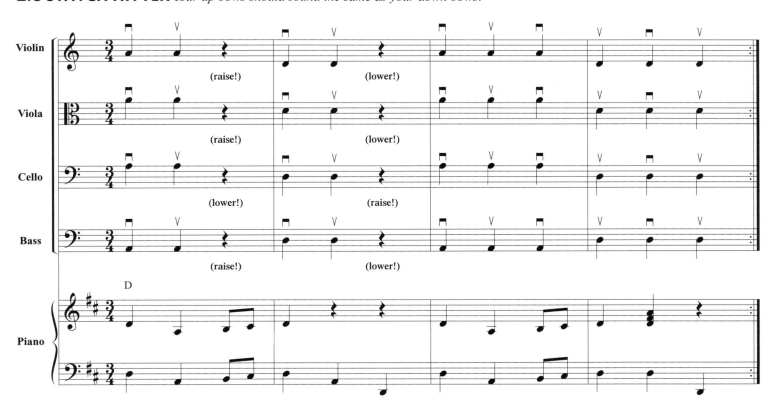

SB307TM

- Encourage students to play full value quarter notes, especially in measures 2 and 4.

- **Extension:** Students can improvise or compose their own pogo stick songs on D and A. Encourage them to explore other string combinations as well as pizzicato and arco techniques.

## 2.9 POGO STICK

### LEFT HAND MEETS RIGHT HAND

You are now ready to combine bowing technique with left-hand fingering!

As you get started, do the following for each exercise:

1. Play *pizzicato*
2. Rosin bow (bass should tube bow)

3. Bow the rhythm on your open D string
4. Put everything together and play as written!

- When bowing fingered notes, it is very important to follow all the above steps. Young children will find the process much easier if you isolate skills, break down the steps, and then put everything together.

COMBINING LEFT AND RIGHT HAND SKILLS

- Continue to check for the following important elements:
  - Bow hold
  - Right shoulder is relaxed and staying down
  - Students are moving from the elbow (violin / viola) or swinging the arm appropriately (cello / bass).

- **Bass tip:** Since bassists are playing an open G, this is an ideal time to remind them that they should be able to see the string vibrate in order to achieve the best sound.

## 2.10 LEFT BRAIN, RIGHT BRAIN

---

REINFORCING LEFT AND RIGHT HAND SKILLS WITH G AND F#

- **Bass tip:** The left hand should be ready to play F# while students are playing open G. Note that fingers do not have to be pressing on the D string, but should be hovering and prepared.

## 2.11 DOWN AND UP Bass *Remember to keep your fingers hovering over the D string while playing open G.*

SB307TM

- Remind students to keep left-hand fingers curved and to keep
  the bow at a right angle with the string.

**2.12 THIRD WHEEL** Bass *Keep your left elbow up so that your wrist is straight.*

### Combining Fingered Notes with Open D

- Whenever the opportunity presents itself, remind students to sit up, check bow holds,
  keep bows at a right angle with the strings, count, and say rests out loud.

**2.13 THREE FOR THREE** *Count and clap before you play.*

**DESCENDING D TETRACHORD**

- **Extension:** To allow for meaningful repetition and to explore expression, consider having students find contrasting ways to go downstairs (borrowing from the title). They can tip-toe (pizzicato), sneak (play softly), stomp (play loudly), etc.

- Have each section play a single measure to encourage independence and counting.

## 2.14 WALKING DOWNSTAIRS

**ASCENDING AND DESCENDING D TETRACHORD**

- Teachers may want to isolate the first two measures since this is the first time students are ascending through the D tetrachord. Consider an echo pattern where the teacher plays the first two measures and students echo. Then the teacher plays the last two measures and students echo.

- **Extension:** Have students listen to the calypso accompaniment. Ask them to visualize where they may be running up and down. Encourage them to play expressively. Are they at the beach? Are they happy? Excited? Tired? Have them try to communicate that thought with the rest of the class!

## 2.15 RUNNING UP AND DOWN Bass *Are your fingers hovering over the D string in measures 2 and 3?*

SB307TM

- This is the first eight-measure tune using the bow. Before and after playing, students should shake out their right hands to release tension. In addition, they can "clap for themselves" by tapping their left thumb against the neck.
- **Cello / Bass tip:** Check regularly to see that the thumb of the left hand is opposite finger 2.

- **Extension:** See if a student can identify the minor tonality of this piece. Explain how this is a good example of how minor can be used in other cultures and is not necessarily 'sad' as is often stereotyped in the United States.

## 2.16 RUSTIC DANCE

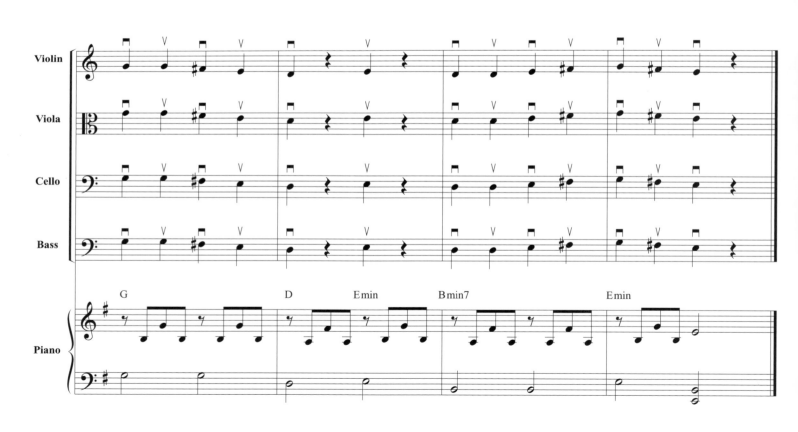

- **Violin / Viola / Cello tip:** Draw comparisons to line 2.10 (same fingering, same rhythm). Ask students to explain what is different about line 2.17.

- **Bass tip:** Check the pitch of high D with open D to make sure they match.

## 2.17 MOVING UP Bass *Keep your left-hand thumb relaxed and behind your 2nd finger when playing in III position.*

### REINFORCING A STRING NOTES WITH THE BOW

- Discuss déjà vu and what it means. Why does this piece have this title? Draw attention to line 2.11 and have students compare and contrast.

## 2.18 DÉJÀ VU

- Remind students to read ahead in the music during the rests.

- Constantly remind students to check their bow hold, violins and violas to move from the elbow, and keep right shoulders relaxed.

**2.19 DOWN THE SCALE** *Say the fingerings for measures 3 and 4 before you play.*

 **THEORY**

## KEY SIGNATURE

The **key signature** indicates which notes to play sharp or flat. It appears at the beginning of each staff.

Your key signature in 2.20, *D Major General,* tells you that all Fs and Cs should be played as F-sharps and C-sharps. While you already know F♯ and C♯, you will no longer see a sharp sign in front of them.

This is the key of **D Major.**

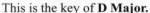
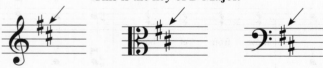

- Since the placement of sharps in the key signature includes lines or spaces of the staff that students may not be familiar with, it may be helpful to review the musical alphabet and have students move up and down the staff to identify the placement of the accidentals in the key signature (see student book page 5).

## D Major Scale with the Bow

- Teach students to use the rests to prepare for the next finger pattern.

### 2.20 D MAJOR GENERAL Bass *Keep your fingers in contact with the G string when shifting.*

- Discuss up bow and down bow patterns, which happen even when they are not marked.

## 2.21 SCALING THE WALL *When bowings are not marked, continue to alternate down and up bows.*

### DESCENDING D MAJOR SCALE WITHOUT RESTS

- If students struggle with 2.21 and 2.22, have them practice without the accompaniment and freeze after playing the A.
- **Teacher tip:** The left-hand fingers should prepare first, then the right arm should change bow levels. Left-hand fingers lead the way for string changes.

- **Extension:** Have students play 2.21 and 2.22 without pause (a complete D major scale that doubles every note).

## 2.22 RAPPELLING DOWN

# RETAKE (BOW LIFT)

A **retake (bow lift)** indicates to lift the bow, circle back to the starting position and set the bow back on the string.

## BOW LIFTS

- Students should practice with small circles first. As before, the shoulder should be relatively still.

- **Bass tip:** Bassists should put the bow on top of the tube so they can lift the bow. The tube can be placed parallel to the strings.

### 2.23 ROCKIN' ROSIN RETAKE Vln./Vla./Cello *Rosin bow. After playing a down bow, lift the bow, circle back to the frog, and set the bow on the rosin.*
**Bass** *Bow on top of the tube. After playing a down bow, lift the bow, circle back to the frog, and set the bow on the tube.*

## BOW LIFTS ON OPEN STRINGS

- When executing bow lifts, have students imagine that the tip of the bow and the frog are drawing imaginary circles in the air. The circles should be the same size! If the frog circle is bigger, students are using too much arm. If the tip circle is bigger, students are flipping the bow out. Strive for equal sized circles!

- The majority of the motion should come from the lower arm and fingers. The shoulder should stay relaxed.

### 2.24 RE-TAKE 2 *Play this exercise on your instrument. Remember to execute the same bow motion during the retake - lift, circle, set!*

SB307TM

- Practice the bowing on open D before playing the music as written.
- Isolate the left hand by playing pizzicato.

- Students should breathe in time during the rest in each measure to help keep pulse.

## 2.25 GIVE AND RETAKE

### COMBINING BOW LIFTS AND SKIPPED NOTES | FRENCH FOLK SONG

- Isolate each measure to practice the skips, particularly measure 3. It may be helpful to isolate each hand (practice on open D and then play pizzicato).
- Make sure violin, viola and cello do not curl the little finger to the side of the fingerboard.

- **Extension:** Have students perform the piece as though they were in an Equestrian competition. They will be judged on tone, posture, intonation, bow hold and the quality of their retakes. Can they clap for themselves with their left thumbs?

## 2.26 WALKING HORSES *How many skips are in this piece?*

French Folk Song

## RHYTHM

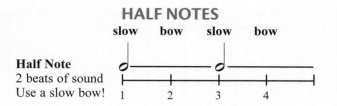

**HALF NOTES**

slow  bow  slow  bow

**Half Note**
2 beats of sound
Use a slow bow!

1   2   3   4

**HALF RESTS**

**Half Rest**
2 beats of silence
(sits on a line)

1   2   =   1   2

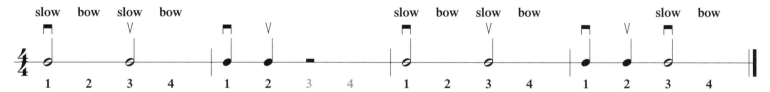

### HALF NOTES AND HALF RESTS | BOW SPEED

- Discuss bow speed. It is helpful for students to internalize "bow" for quarter notes and "slow bow" for half notes.
- Young string players do not need to use the extremes of the bow at this time because this could affect their bow angle.

- Students should count while rosin / tube bowing. This will help them count the half rests as well as the half notes.
- Make sure students keep their bow parallel to the bridge for the entire note. Some may pull their bow to the side.

**2.27 BOW BEAT** **Vln./Vla.** *Rosin bow the rhythm. Be sure to keep your shoulders low and open from the elbow.*
*Use a slow bow on half notes!*
**Cello/Bass** *Rosin (tube) bow the rhythm. Be sure to keep your shoulders low and swing from the elbow.*
*Use a slow bow on half notes!*

slow bow slow bow    slow bow slow bow    slow bow    slow bow

### HALF NOTES | HALF RESTS

- Students can count out loud to help play the half notes full value (and rest for full value as well).

- **Extension:** Have students memorize this exercise and play it while watching carefully where the bow contacts the string. Have them critique themselves.

### 2.28 HALFTIME

SB307TM

- Have students play this piece one of two ways:
  - Putting the baby to sleep
  - Waking the baby up

- Have them play for a partner or the class. Can others guess the musical intent of the performer?

**2.29 SLEEPING BABY** Bass *Remember to keep your thumb relaxed and flat behind the neck.*

French Folk Song

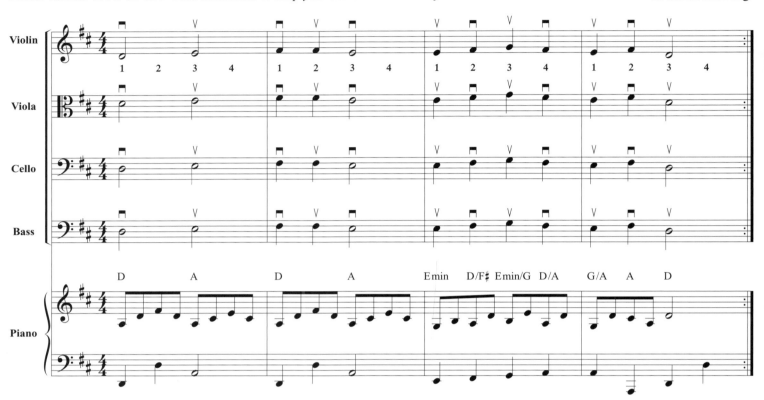

STUDENT PAGE **17**

 THEORY

## FIRST AND SECOND ENDINGS

At the first ending, play through to the repeat sign. Go back to the beginning or the previous repeat sign and play again. Now skip the first ending – play the second ending instead.

FIRST AND SECOND ENDINGS | D TETRACHORD AND OPEN A

- Before playing, have students use a finger to track the music and follow the road map, demonstrating knowledge of first and second endings.
- Students should keep their fingers hovering over the D string when they move to the A string.

**2.30 JINGLE BELLS** **Bass** *Practice measure 3 alone, moving only your 1st finger to play A while your other fingers hover over the D string.*

James Pierpont

*hop!*

- This exercise will be useful for evaluating understanding of half notes.
- This is also a good exercise to discuss and plan bow distribution.

- **Extension:** Revisit the discussion about waltzes (originally mentioned in 2.6 *Waltz of the Bows*). Have students tap left foot on beat one and right foot on beats 2 and 3.
- Discuss the unexpected use of half and quarter notes in the first 4 measures. Clowns are known for doing the unexpected!

## 2.31 CIRCUS CLOWN

**THEORY**

# DUET

A **duet** has two different parts performed simultaneously by two individuals or groups.

DUET

- All students should learn the A and B parts individually.
- Emphasize that a duet is two people playing two *different* parts. Many students think that both playing a melody together at the same time is a duet.

- Have students memorize and play with a friend while facing each other.

**2.32 TWO FOR ONE - Duet** *Practice playing both parts of this duet.*

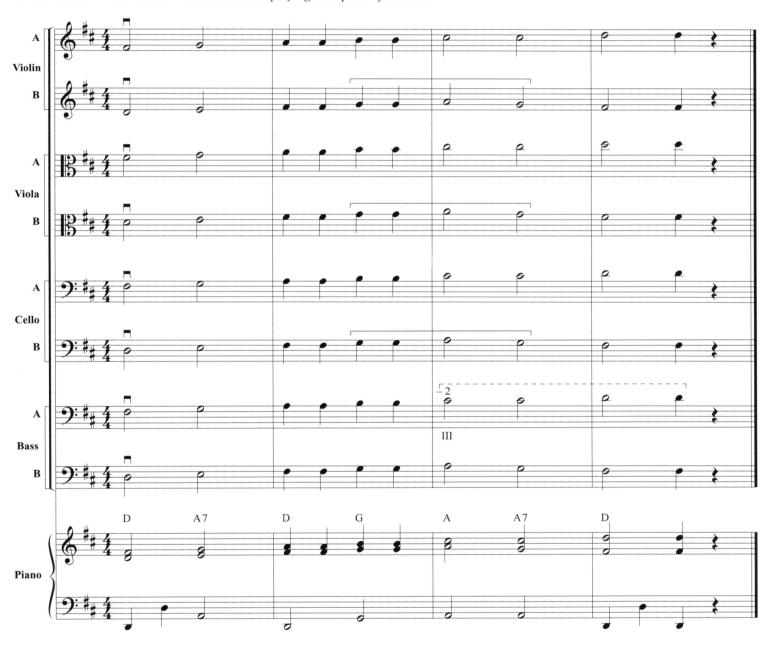

## THEORY

## TEMPO MARKINGS

**Tempo** is the speed of the beat. Music can move at different rates of speed.

**Andante** - a slow, walking tempo     **Moderato** - a medium tempo     **Allegro** - a fast tempo

- In addition to discussing different rates of speed, discuss how this affects bow speed and distribution (slower music = slower bow speed).

### DUET | FIRST AND SECOND ENDINGS | ALLEGRO

- Practice B to A (first ending) and B to G (second ending) away from the music. Have students identify where skips occur in the music.
- Remind students to read ahead and THINK (prepare) during rests!
- Point out the tempo marking. Ask students to explain what it means.

- **Extension:** For a truly epic experience, play the piece three times.
  - First time, play the A part only.
  - Second time, play the B part only.
  - Third time (for the grand finale), put the parts together and feel the excitement! Can students make the excitement build the entire time? If so, how? Discuss what they are doing to change the sound.

### 2.33 EPIC - Duet

## Hopping Between Strings (1st finger)

- Practice hopping between E and B without music. Gradually work up tempo until students are able to play the first measure.
- Notice that this is marked pizzicato so students can focus on the left hand.

- **Bass tip:** Bassists need to keep the hand open when playing 1st finger on the D string and 4th finger on the G string. Encourage them to keep 1st finger on D while fingers 2, 3 and 4 remain on the G string. This technique will take a while to develop, but it is important to make students aware of it early.

**2.34 HOP AROUND** Vln./Vla./Cello *When changing from E to B, your first finger should lift completely off the D string and "hop" over to the A string.*

*Bass Keep your first finger on the D string while preparing fingers 2, 3 and 4 to move over to play on the G string.*

- Point out the tempo marking and discuss.
- Sing the chant with letter names.

**2.35 CHANT** Vln./Vla./Cello *Remember to hop between each E and B in measures 1 and 2!*
Bass *Keep your hand open and relaxed when going between E and B.*

**HISTORY**

## MUSIC
**Pyotr Ilyich Tchaikovsky** (1840–1893) was a Russian composer whose famous works include the *1812 Overture* and *The Nutcracker*. Ironically, *The Nutcracker* was not originally a success, and it was only later that it became one of his most famous compositions.

## SCIENCE
In 1893, African-American surgeon Daniel Hale Williams performed one of the first successful open heart surgeries. Later that year, the Johns Hopkins Medical School opened in Baltimore, Maryland.

## WORLD
Thomas Edison completed construction of the world's first motion picture studio in West Orange, New Jersey. In Germany, Karl Friedrich Benz received a patent for a gas-powered automobile and eventually founded Mercedes-Benz.

- **Extension:** Play excerpts from *The Nutcracker, 1812 Overture,* and other Tchaikovsky pieces that students may know. Discuss science and world history happening at the same time Tchaikovsky was writing music.

- Practice finger hops and bow lifts away from the music
- Identify the tempo marking and ask students to explain its meaning.

- Play pizzicato, then rosin / tube bow, and finally put it all together.

## 2.36 OVERTURE TO THE NUTCRACKER

Pyotr I. Tchaikovsky

# OPUS 2 ENCORE

## INTERPRETATION STATION

*Interpretation Station* focuses on students' ability to listen to and make judgments about performance, style, expression, and contrasts.

- In this assessment, we focus on the student's ability to listen to and critique performances. While designed as part of a unit assessment, this particular assessment can be used anytime.
- Students should listen to the two performances in class or at home and write a journal entry critiquing the two performances.

- Encourage students to make music-specific comments using vocabulary they have learned.

Listen to the corresponding track on the DVD. You will hear two performances of the same piece. Which one is better and why?

**Music:** *Postcards from Russia* arranged by Carrie Lane Gruselle.

## SIMON SEZ

*Simon "Sez"* is an assessment of the development of aural skills. Performance skills gained from reading are discrete and different from performance skills guided by aural cues.

Below is a transcription of the melody students hear on the CD. Students, however, do not have anything in their books.

- Teachers may choose to supplement with their own echo patterns that are tailored for the ability of their students.
- Have students critique themselves and each other. *Did they match the recording?*

Listen to the corresponding track on the DVD. You will hear a series of four-note patterns. Listen to the patterns and echo them back. *Hint: the first pattern starts on your open D string!*

## COMPOSER'S CORNER

*Composer's Corner* allows you to assess students' ability to transfer skills acquired from exercises specific to each Opus into a created product. It is a synthesis exercise to help you assess higher order thinking.

- Students may complete this particular assessment at any time during the Opus.
- Encourage students to perform their piece for a partner, the class, or their family.

- Consider repeating the assessment as the students learn new notes.

Use the notes and rhythms you have learned to complete the composition. When you are finished, add your own bowings!

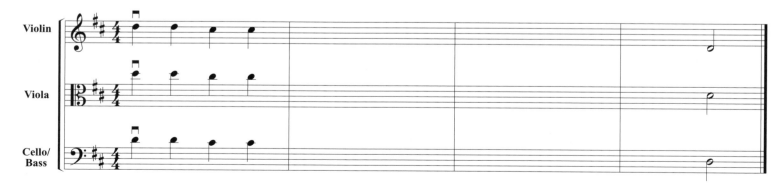

## PENCIL POWER

*Pencil Power* assessments allow you to assess students' ability to identify certain musical concepts generally found in the written score. It also assesses broader musical knowledge.

Match the following terms with their definitions.

**1.** _____ Retake     **5.** _____ Arco

**2.** _____ Allegro     **6.** _____ Pizzicato

**3.** _____ Andante     **7.** _____ Moderato

**4.** _____ Duet     **8.** _____ Accidental

**A.** A medium tempo

**B.** Pluck the string

**C.** A sign placed to the left of a note that alters its pitch

**D.** A piece with two different parts performed simultaneously

**E.** A fast tempo

**F.** An indication to lift the bow and circle back to the starting position

**G.** A slow, walking tempo

**H.** Bow the string

**Answer Key:**   1. F   2. E   3. G   4. D   5. H   6. B   7. A   8. C

## CURTAIN UP!

The *Curtain Up!* section includes a performance piece covering material that has been reviewed in Opus 2. Students should be encouraged to use the CD and give full performances for friends and family. This is also a time to learn performance and concert etiquette. Students should introduce each piece by title and acknowledge applause by bowing.

### ASSESSMENT OF SKILLS PRESENTED IN OPUS 2

- Teachers should look for the following elements:
  1. Proper playing position
  2. Left-hand fingers are curved and wrist is straight
  3. Bow hold
  4. Bow stroke (perpendicular to the string)
  5. Retake (tip and frog are making similar size circles)
  6. Bow distribution on half notes
  7. Understanding of tempo marking

Note: This piece appears on two lines in the student books, but has been consolidated here to eliminate a page turn.

## 2.37 TRIFECTA

## BOW-NUS!

The *Bow-Nus!* section focuses on bow technique. This is an ideal time to offer extra credit or encourage further right-hand development. Encourage students to practice small bow lifts on open strings before practicing the piece as written.

SMALL BOW LIFTS | 3/4 TIME

**2.38 WELCOME THE HEROES** *There are times when you need to do a retake without a rest present. Work on playing as full a quarter note as possible, then do a small lift / circle before your next down bow.*

# CURTAIN UP!  FIRST CONCERT

Beginning with Opus 2, every chapter includes string orchestra performance music. In Opus 2, each student book has two pages of music that include a warm-up, original music and arrangements, rounds, and holiday music. These pieces are ideal to use in a first concert setting.

## ROUND

In a **round**, each musician or group plays the same part, but enters at a different time.

- Review the definition of a round. Have the entire ensemble play in unsion before splitting into different groups. Try playing it as a 3 part round in addition to a 2 part round.

**2.39 D MAJOR SCALE - Round** *As a group reaches* ②*, the next group should begin playing at* ① *.*

- All orchestra arrangements include A, B and C parts.
  - A = melody
  - B = harmony
  - C = bass line
- All instruments contain the A line. Violin and viola also have the B (harmony) line while cello and bass have the C (bass) line.

- **Extension:** This is a great opportunity to discuss other women composers.
  - Suggested reading: *Women and Music* by Karin Pendle (Indiana University Press)

## 2.40 LOVE THE SUN - Orchestra Arrangement
## (from "Liebst du um Schonheit")

Clara Schumann
arr. Carrie Lane Gruselle

- Encourage the students to come up with a story for this piece. They can create words to go along with the tune.

- For a special challenge, have students switch parts on the repeat.

## 2.41 DEFENDERS OF EARTH - Orchestra Arrangement

Brian Balmages

- Practice playing A to D (measure 3) away from the music at first. Be sure the finger for C# lands in the correct place when the fingers go down for D.

- However you divide the class, be sure each half gets the opportunity to play both parts.

Note: This piece appears on two lines in the student books, but has been consolidated here to eliminate a page turn.

## 2.42 ALL THE WOODS ARE WAKING - Round

American Folk Song

- However you divide the class, be sure each section gets the opportunity to play the melody line.

## 2.43 HOLIDAYS UNITED! - Orchestra Arrangement

arr. Brian Balmages

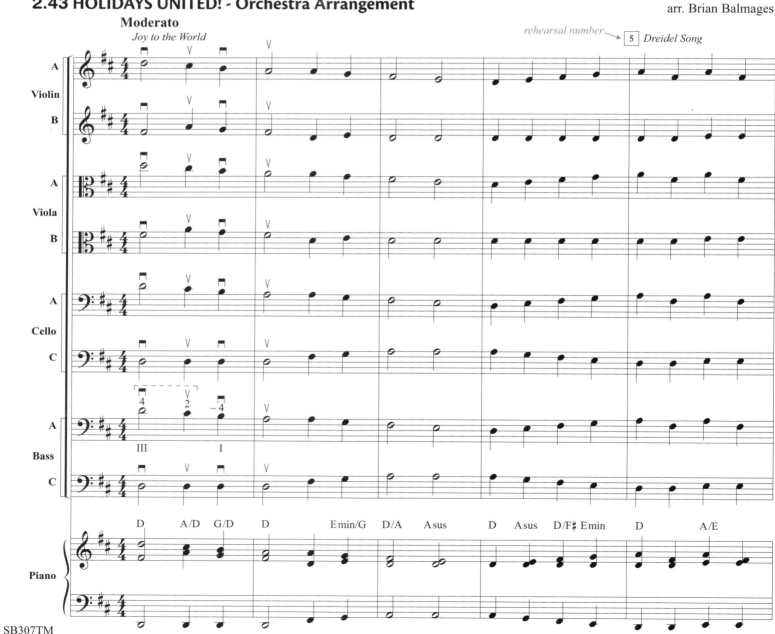

• Cello and bass players can slap strings and fingerboard during the rests in the bass (C) line.

## 2.44 DOWN ON THE FARM - Orchestra Arrangement

American Folk Song
arr. Carrie Lane Gruselle

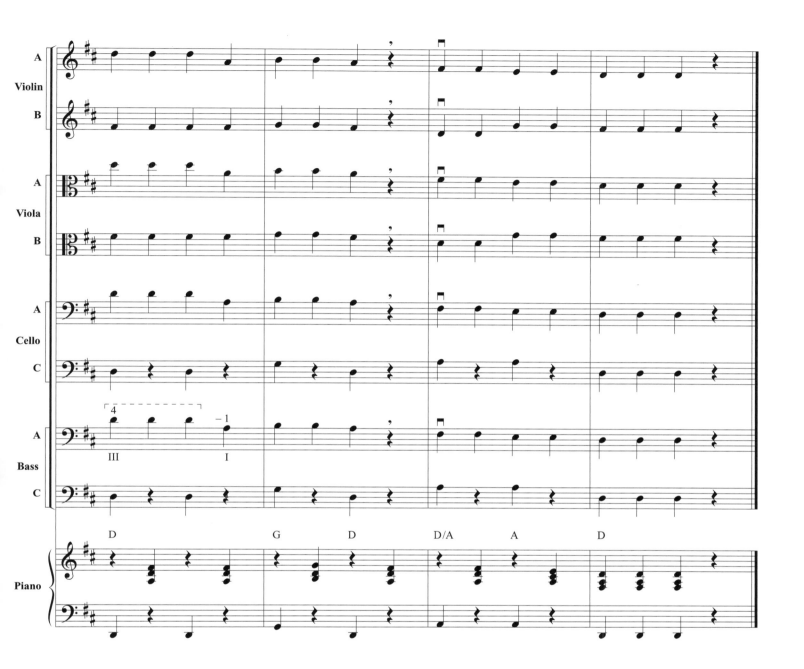

# OPUS 3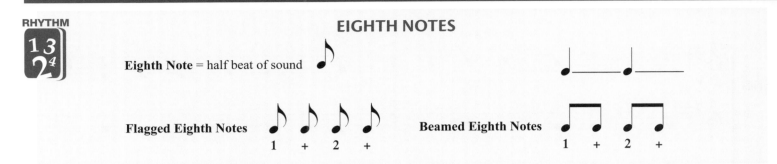

## EIGHTH NOTES

**Eighth Note** = half beat of sound

**Flagged Eighth Notes**

1 + 2 +

**Beamed Eighth Notes**

1 + 2 +

## EIGHTH NOTES

- Whichever counting system you use in the classroom, be sure the students are verbalizing the eighth notes.
- We have used the 1-and-2-and system for simplicity, but you can use Takadimi or Gordon's rhythm syllables if you prefer. For efficiency and meaningful transfer, it may be useful to use the same counting system as your school's general music teacher.
- Have students play this exercise both pizzicato and arco on open D.

- Divide the class into three sections. One section plays four measures of quarter notes on D string, the second group plays four measures of eighth notes on F♯ and the third group plays 3.1 as written on the A string. This strategy can be used on many exercises in this book.
- **Extension:** Play each measure on a different string!

### 3.1 BOW BEAT *Rosin (tube) bow.*

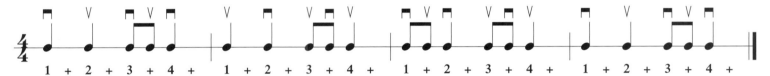

## EIGHTH NOTES IN MUSIC

- Students should compare this exercise to 3.1 How is it alike? How is it different?
- Clap, pizzicato, then play with the bow!

- **Bass tip:** Reinforce that students will no longer see brackets when they shift positions.

### 3.2 EIGHTH NOTE CHA-CHA-CHA

EIGHTH NOTES | MODERATO | BOW DISTRIBUTION

- Use almost a full bow for quarter notes and a smaller, faster bow for eighth notes.
- Basses will use less bow on quarter notes than the other instruments.

- **Extension:** Who are the nobles? What makes this a noble melody? How can students perform to make it even more noble sounding?

## 3.3 ENTRY OF THE NOBLES

# BEAM GROUPS

## EIGHTH NOTES BEAMED IN GROUPS OF FOUR

- Have students compare measures 1 and 3 (or ask them which measures have the same rhythm but are notated differently).

- Discuss and demonstrate the different speeds and parts of the bow necessary for this rhythm.

- Have students use one note of the D or A tetrachord for each measure (i.e. D | E | F♯ | G, or A | B | C♯ | D).

### 3.4 BOW BEAT *Rosin (tube) bow.*

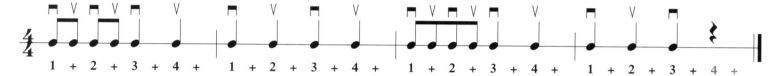

## EIGHTH NOTE REINFORCEMENT WITH TEXT

- Have students sing before playing.

- Identify measures that sound alike but are notated differently.

- **Extension:** Have students improvise a duet line on open D and A using the rhythm of the tune.

## 3.5 PIZZA ON THE RIVER!

**RHYTHM**
**13**
**2/4**

## TIME SIGNATURE

**2** **2 beats** in each measure
**4** Quarter note gets one beat

## CONDUCTING IN 2/4 TIME

It is your turn to conduct!
Using your right hand, follow
the diagram to conduct in 2/4 time.

- Having students conduct makes them more aware of your gestures.

- Play examples of music in 2/4 time (such as marches). It helps them to hear examples.

### INTRODUCTION TO 2/4 TIME

- Review time signatures. What does the top number indicate? What about the bottom number? Relate to 4/4 time.
- How is it possible to have 3 notes in 2/4 time?
- As with 3.1 and 3.4, have students play the exercise pizzicato, then bow on different open strings. Finally, add the left hand and create melodic fragments.

- Divide class into three sections. One section plays four measures of quarter notes on D string, the second group plays four measures of eighth notes on F# and the third group plays 3.6 as written on the A string.

### 3.6 BOW BEAT *Rosin (tube) bow.*

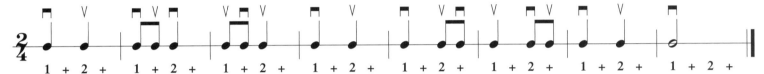

### REINFORCING 2/4 TIME

- Compare 3.6 and 3.7

- Play pizzicato before playing arco.

### 3.7 FIDDLE STICKS **Bass** *Look for position changes before you play!*

American Folk Song

THEORY

# THEME AND VARIATIONS

Composers create a **variation** when they change a melody in some way. While you will hear the differences in each variation, you will still be able to recognize the original theme.

- Lines 3.8 through 3.10 are used to illustrate theme and variations. Discuss variations in time signature and rhythm while also showing consistency in melody.

---

**THEME | EIGHTH NOTES | D TETRACHORD | 2/4 TIME | DOUBLE STOPS (VIOLIN / VIOLA / CELLO)**

- Encourage violin, viola and cello students to add the A string to create a double stop.
  - Check for long fingernails, which will get in the way and affect the double stops. The double stops will take a few trials, but you can make it fun for them by comparing it to Bluegrass fiddling. Remind the violin and viola students that left hand fingers are pulled into correct position by the left elbow. As you pull the left elbow to your right, it will pull the fingertips to your left. This is exactly what you want! Try it!
  - Encourage violin and viola students to S-T-R-E-T-C-H the 2nd finger away from the 1st finger to get the whole step perfectly in tune. Some teachers like to have students listen for a ringing sound. Double stops are a great aid in hearing this.

- Encourage all students to make the tunnel over the A string so that fingers do not touch the A.
- **Cello tip:** Cellists can also play the double stops, keeping fingers arched and on their tips. If students have weak knuckles that tend to collapse on F♯, this is a chance to strengthen them.
- **Bass tip 1:** Remind bassists to keep fingers close to the D string (hovering or lightly touching the string) when going to open G.
- **Bass extension:** Using only their open D, G and A strings, have bassists improvise a bass line for this piece.

## 3.8 BOIL THEM CABBAGE DOWN

**Vln./Vla./Cello** *Bow-nus! Bowing two strings at the same time is called a **double stop**. With your finger tunnels in place, play this exercise while also playing your open A string!*
**Cello** *Bow-nus! Bowing two strings at the same time is called a **double stop**. Play this exercise while also playing your open A string!*

**Vln.** *After playing 3.8, go back and play 3.7 Fiddle Sticks while also playing your E string!*

- Be sure violinists and violists open from the right elbow rather than bow from the shoulder.
  - Encourage students to have the right-hand 1st finger square up over the A string so that it does not touch that string.
- Cellists and bassists should focus on unfolding the right arm.
- Have the violin and viola students pull their left arms well under the violin in playing position until a small portion is visible inside the C bout of the instrument.
  - S-T-R-E-T-C-H the 1st and 2nd fingers until they form the shape of two tunnels (call them overpasses if you prefer).

- Tapping with the left thumb against the neck is a useful way to release tension for all instruments. Have students clap for themselves often with their left thumbs!
- Repeated reminders to play only on the tips of the fingers will be necessary.
- **Cello tip:** Cellists should be reminded to balance the bow over both A and D strings, and sink into both strings with a heavy bow arm. Is the right thumb bent and the left thumb relaxed? Clap for yourself with your left thumb!
- **Bass tip:** Remind basses to keep fingers close on D string (hovering or lightly touching string) when going to the open G string.

## 3.9 THREE CABBAGES (Variation 1) Vln./Vla./Cello *Bow-nus! Play double stops on the D and A strings!*

SB307TM

• Students should play the eighth notes near the balance point of the bow, but pull a longer, faster bow on quarter notes.

## 3.10 CABBAGES GALORE! (Variation 2) Vln./Vla./Cello *Bow-nus! Play double stops!*

# LEFT-HAND PIZZICATO

+ Play pizzicato with your left-hand 4th finger

**Vln./Vla.** Be sure to keep your wrist straight and your left elbow under the instrument.

## LEFT-HAND (4TH-FINGER) PIZZICATO

- Plucking the string with 4th finger will help strengthen that finger.

- Violin and viola students will find this easier if they pull their left elbows slightly to the right while rotating their wrists slightly to the left, thus moving their 4th finger toward the lower strings.

**3.11 4th FINGER MARCH** **Vln./Vla.** *Make sure you do not collapse the wrist as you play 4th-finger pizzicato. Is your left elbow under the violin / viola?*

**Cello** *Make sure you do not collapse the wrist as you play 4th- finger pizzicato.*

- Watch to be sure upper string players keep their wrists aligned with their lower arms (rather than bumping out or collapsing their wrists).
- **Violin / Viola tip:** Have students make a 4th-finger tunnel over the A string.

- To ease the coordination challenge, instruct the students to have their bows rest on the D string while plucking the A string.

## 3.12 LITTLE FINGER WALTZ

**The following information and exercises appear in the bass book only and prepares students for 3.13.**
**Students should play each exercise in first position before playing in third position.**

SHIFTING

## THIRD (III) POSITION
## ON THE D STRING

Up until now, you have been playing in third position on the G string only. Using third position on the D string allows you to avoid some string crossings and play more musically.

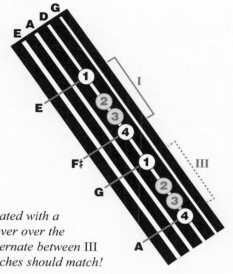

### 3.12a FINDING G IN III - Basses Only

*Stay in III position where indicated with a bracket. Your fingers should hover over the string when not being used. Alternate between III position G and open G. The pitches should match!*

### 3.12b I TO III AND BACK ON D - Basses Only

*Make sure your thumb is relaxed and stays behind your 2nd finger when you shift.*

### 3.12c DÉJÀ VU - Basses Only

*Even though you are shifting to III position, measures 3 and 4 should sound the*

- Using III position on the D string will help with intonation. In addition, students can now easily play G and A without leaving III position. Have them revisit 1.23 *Groovin' Grandma* on student page 8 (TM page 50) to see how much easier it is to stay in    III position!

# VIOLIN
## 4th-FINGER A (ON THE D STRING)

Using 4th-finger A on the D string allows for smoother technique and a richer sound in appropriate places. You can check your intonation (being in tune) by comparing it to your open A. Keep your wrist straight and your left elbow under the violin.

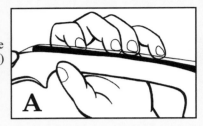

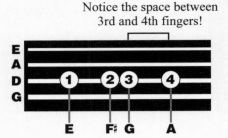

Notice the space between 3rd and 4th fingers!

# VIOLA
## 4th-FINGER A (ON THE D STRING)

Using 4th-finger A on the D string allows for smoother technique and a richer sound in appropriate places. You can check your intonation (being in tune) by comparing it to your open A. Keep your wrist straight and your left elbow under the viola.

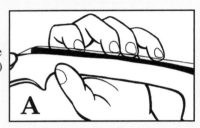

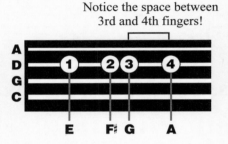

Notice the space between 3rd and 4th fingers!

SHIFTING

# CELLO
## BOW-NUS: 2nd POSITION

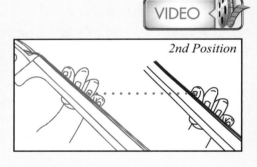

*2nd Position*

Up until now, you have been playing in 1st position. To play in **2nd position**, shift your left hand down so that your 1st finger is now on F♯. Your thumb should also move, staying behind your 2nd finger. You will add 2nd finger for G, and all four fingers to play A. Make sure your thumb stays relaxed when you shift between 1st and 2nd positions.

Roman numerals (I and II) are used to indicate when you shift positions. In addition, a dash is always put in front of the first fingering in a new position.

• Second position for cello is optional in this book, yet is ideal for motivated students to learn while upper strings learn 4th-finger A. Optional II position fingerings are indicated under the music throughout the book.

- **Cello tip:** When shifting, be sure that the left thumb glides along the neck without squeezing. The thumb should land behind finger 2 (note G).

- **Cello / Bass tip:** Students can check the accuracy of the shift by playing in first position as well. Some may perceive the tone or timbre difference as a difference in pitch. This may take some demonstration to address pitch differences versus tone differences.

### 3.13 TWO-WAY A
*Vln./Vla. Keep your fingers down while going to the A string. Is your 4th finger A in tune with your open A?*
**Cello** *Bow-nus! While you can play this entirely in 1st position, try shifting to 2nd position where indicated.*
**Bass** *Keep your fingers down on the D string where indicated with a solid bracket.*

- **Cello tip:** If the shift to II position is difficult, students can play in I position. If the students are motivated to improve their shifting, they can continue to study 3.13 and later add the shift into 3.14 when they feel secure.

- **Bass tip:** As with other similar exercises, bassists can play the exercise entirely in I position before practicing the shift to III position.

### 3.14 HURON CAROL
**Cello** *Bow-nus! Shift to 2nd position where indicated!*

French-Canadian Hymn

SB307TM

**4**

## COMMON TIME

**c** The **common time** symbol means the same thing as 4/4 time.

## CONDUCTING IN 4/4 TIME

It is your turn to conduct! Using your right hand, follow the diagram to conduct in 4/4 time.

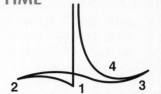

REINFORCING 4TH-FINGER A | COMMON TIME | II POSITION (CELLO) | III POSITION (BASS)

- Students will need to have good 4th-finger contact with the string for eighth notes to sound clearly.
- Encourage students to persist. The sound will be brighter as finger strength develops with practice.

### 3.15 FIDDLIN' 4th FINGER Cello *Bow-nus! Shift to 2nd position where indicated!*

**The following exercises appear in the bass book and reinforce third position on both the D and G strings.**

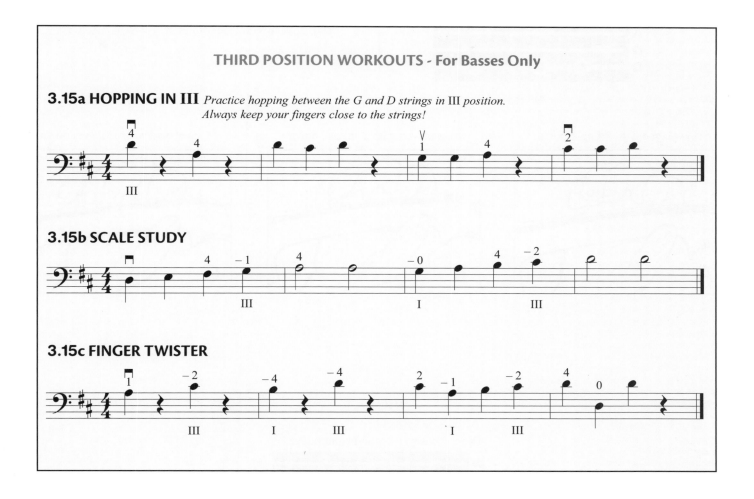

SB307TM

# VIOLIN

## NOTES ON THE G STRING
(Keep your wrist straight and relaxed)

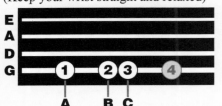

## LEDGER LINES

**Ledger lines** extend the staff. Notes written above or below the staff appear with ledger lines.

A is played with 1 finger down

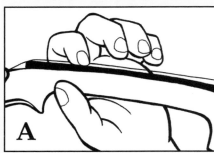

B is played with 2 fingers down

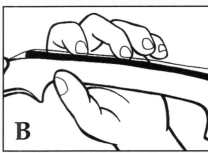

C is played with 3 fingers down

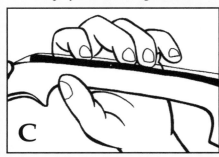

# VIOLA

## NOTES ON THE G STRING
(Keep your wrist straight and relaxed)

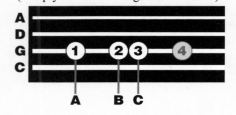

A is played with 1 finger down

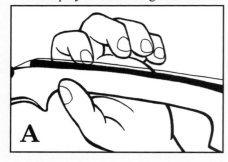

B is played with 2 fingers down

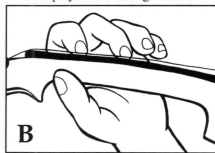

C is played with 3 fingers down

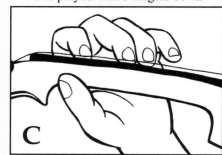

## CELLO

### NOTES ON THE G STRING
(Keep your wrist straight and relaxed)

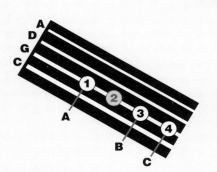

A is played with 1 finger down

B is played with 3 fingers down

C is played with 4 fingers down

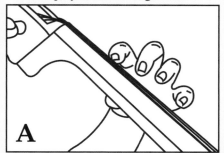

A

B

C

## DOUBLE BASS
## NEW NOTE: G

G is played with 2 fingers down
on the E string

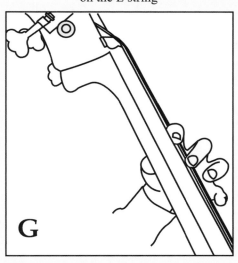

G

**3.15d TUNE THIS TUNE - Basses Only** *Your fingers should hover over the E string when they are not down.*

- This is a preparatory exercise for 3.16.

- Remind bassists to keep 1st and 2nd fingers hovering above low G while playing open G and A. Students should compare low G with open G.

- **Violin / Viola tip:** Keep the right arm and elbow just high enough that the bow hairs do not touch the D string, but not so high as to rub the bout near the G string on the violin, or touch the C string on viola.

  - As always, students should pull the down bow from the elbow to start, but let the entire right arm be flexible to help keep the bow straight. Work hard to keep thumb and pinkie curved and on their tips. This may be more challenging than the students may think, so give it plenty of attention.

  - Be careful that students do not play on the G string with the right hand really high and the right elbow really low (close to the rib cage). Not all violinists agree on how high or low

to keep the right elbow when playing on the G string, but a good beginner's compromise is to keep the entire bow arm fairly level, lowering and raising it only as much as necessary. *Avoid raising and lowering the right hand and bow while leaving the elbow close to the rib cage!*

- **Cello tip:** Cellists will relax their bow arm, check the bow hold with a bent thumb, and let the arm weight sink into the G string. Have enough weight for the G to ring freely, but not so much that the bow bumps neighboring strings. This might be a good time to discuss and demonstrate the concept of "dead weight" – arm weight with no pressure.

- **Bass tip:** Remind students that less bow is needed for lower pitches.

## 3.16 G FOR ME

NEW NOTE: A / FIRST FINGER ON G STRING (VIOLIN / VIOLA / CELLO) | REINFORCING G (BASS)

- **Violin / Viola tip:** Keep the first finger of the left hand squared off and arched over all strings. Letting the left knuckle square off over all the strings will make playing the violin or viola much easier!

  - *Students should not let the finger flatten!* A squared finger is strong, quick and flexible!

- If students are reluctant to maintain a good hand position, you may want to demonstrate vibrato and shifting into upper positions to let them know what lies ahead. It is important to establish good hand position from the start.

- **Bass tip:** Students should prepare low G before beginning.

**3.17 DARK WATERS** Vln./Vla./Cello *Keep your first finger down where indicated!*

- **Teacher's note:** Notes on the G string are introduced gradually. Students will spend several exercises playing tunes that use G and A as extensions of pieces otherwise playable on D and A strings. This allows for more focus on each note and better reading / comprehension.

- Play the piece in unison before dividing the class into groups.

- Listen for an especially bright sound on the F# in the opening phrase. Let the class take turns playing F# too low so they can hear how dreary it sounds compared with when it is in tune.

- Practice eighth note fingerings very slowly for accuracy of pitch and coordination of the bow, fingers, and string crossings. If necessary, make a repeating exercise out of measures 9 – 10 and have the class repeat it slowly. You may have to repeat this slowly several times before speeding it up. If it goes well a little faster, give lots of praise and applaud the class for their diligence.

- A weak 4th finger sounds very much like a flat 4th finger (as in pitch). Examine carefully to determine if the finger is actually too low, or if it is simply not pressing the string fully against the fingerboard. A lot of finger pressure is not necessary, so caution students against squeezing the pinkie too hard.

- **Violin / Viola / Cello tip:** Leave the first finger on the G string when crossing to the D string in measures 13 and 15.

- **Violin / Viola tip:** Keep 2nd and 3rd fingers down on D string to strengthen the 4th.

  - Note that some teachers allow those students who struggle with 4th fingers to release the 1st finger and pull the hand ever so slightly closer to the bridge (no more than a fraction of an inch). Students return the hand to its correct placement by the time the 1st finger is needed. Some teachers oppose this, but it may improve 4th finger accuracy for those unable to reach from 1 to 4 easily and accurately. Next year (or even next month), these fingers will probably be longer and stronger. Be sure these students are pulling their left elbows well under the instruments.

- **Cello tip:** Those who are having success with shifting may want to play measures 5 – 8 in second position (1, 2, 4).

- **Bass tip:** Students can play this entirely in first position before practicing the shift.

## 3.18 FRÉRE JACQUES - Round

French Folk Song

**The following three exercises appear in the bass book and introduce II position while also preparing students for 3.19. In all cases, students should play the exercise in I position prior to practicing it in II position.**

## SECOND (II) POSITION

To play in **second position**, shift your left hand so that your 2nd finger moves to F♯ on the D string (where you have been putting your 4th finger down for F♯). Remember that your thumb should also move, staying relaxed and behind your 2nd finger. You can now play G with your 4th finger! Practice playing 4th finger G (second position) and open G. The pitches should match.

Roman numeral II indicates when you shift to second position.

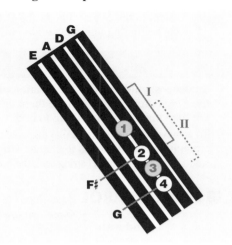

Note: The following exercises that use second position can ALSO be played in first position!

### 3.18a II FOR YOU - Basses Only *Match your F♯ in I position with your F♯ in II position.*

### 3.18b THE MATCHING GAME - Basses Only *Practice so that measures 3 and 4 sound exactly like measures 1 and 2!*

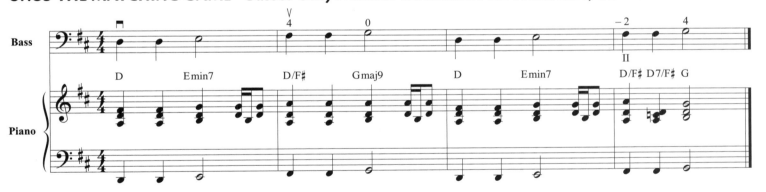

### 3.18c ALMOST FRENCH - Basses Only

SB307TM

**THEORY**

## D.C. AL FINE

**D.C.** is an abbreviation for *da capo,* an Italian term that refers to the beginning. At the **D.C. al Fine,** return to the beginning and play again until the **Fine** (the end).

## DOUBLE BAR LINE

A **double bar line** indicates the end of one section and the beginning of another.

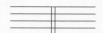

### D.C. al Fine | Double Bar Line | Legato String Crossing

- Students should identify the location of the *D.C. al Fine* and the *Fine* before playing. Have them use their finger to track the road map from beginning to end.

- To achieve a *legato* style of playing, students should minimize the amount their arm moves to change strings. For example, get students to play on the G string with the bow as close to the D string

as possible (without sounding it). This will make playing smooth and connected.

- **Extension:** To hear students individually or to feature soloists on a concert, repeat the piece in its entirety as many times as you wish. Have full ensemble play measures 1-8 while a soloist or small group plays measures 9-12. For variety, have students make decisions about dynamic contrasts.

## 3.19 FRENCH CAROL Bass *Begin by practicing only the measures that use II position. Once you are ready, play the entire piece.*

Traditional

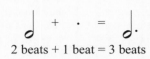

## THE RULE OF THE DOT

Adding a dot after a note increases the length of the note by half its value. When adding a dot to a half note, it becomes a **dotted half note**. Use a slower bow (even slower than a half note!).

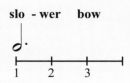

2 beats + 1 beat = 3 beats

## CONDUCTING IN $\frac{3}{4}$ TIME

Practice conducting in $\frac{3}{4}$ time!

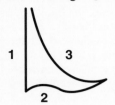

---

### DOTTED HALF NOTE

- Students should think (and say) "slo-wer bow" steadily over the three beats of the dotted half note. Contrast this with "slow bow," which is how they should be internalizing the half note. This should help with bow distribution.

- Have half the class play dotted half notes while the other half plays quarter notes. Switch.

### 3.20 BOW BEAT *Rosin (tube) bow*

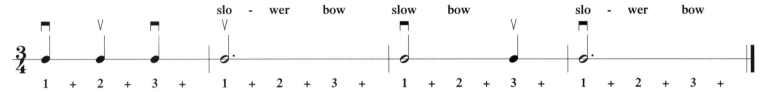

---

### REINFORCING DOTTED HALF NOTES | D TETRACHORD

- Reinforce the use of "slo-wer bow" and "slow bow." Replace with counting.

### 3.21 GETTING A HANDLE ON IT!

**HISTORY**

## MUSIC

**George F. Handel** (1685–1759) was a German-born composer who composed operas, oratorios, orchestral works and more. *Music for the Royal Fireworks* was written when George II of Great Britain hired him to compose music to accompany fireworks in London to commemorate the signing of the Treaty of Aix-la-Chapelle in 1749.

## SCIENCE

Sir Isaac Newton, English physicist and mathematician, proposed the laws of motion and universal gravitation. He demonstrated that the motion of objects on Earth and in space could be described by the same principles. He became known as one of the greatest scientists of all time.

## WORLD

The Treaty of Aix-la-Chapelle ended the War of the Austrian Succession. The war involved most of the major powers in Europe and centered around the House of Habsburg, whose head was often elected as emperor of the Holy Roman Empire.

- This is a good opportunity to relate other world events occurring when Handel was composing music for George II of Great Britain.

---

### DOTTED HALF NOTE | MAESTOSO | COMBINING THREE STRINGS

- Encourage students to conserve bow and lighten arm weight on the half notes to prevent an unintentional 'lurch' on the up-bow. Sing "slow-bow, up! slow-bow, up!"
- Demonstrate and/or sing the *maestoso* style. Clarify the best area of the bow to use and which notes to separate. Remind students that this music was written for a king and they should use especially good posture and position. Consider

adding percussion parts and inviting beginning band percussionists to join in.

- **Bass tip:** Students may want to play this piece in first position before practicing it with the shift (Remember that students do not have to use II position in this book, but it is very practical and helpful).

---

### 3.22 MUSIC FOR THE ROYAL FIREWORKS Vln./Vla./Cello *Prepare the 1st finger on the G string before you begin.*

George F. Handel

- **Violin / Viola tip:** Watch 4th fingers particularly in the first measure, where they may tend to curl up near the E string side of the neck. Encourage students to keep the 4th finger in its "ready" position, hovering just above the string and ready to instantly drop down on the string (just like the other fingers!).

- **Cello tip:** Check left-hand and arm position on the first note. Is the left forearm level with the back of the hand? The level at which the arm is raised will be determined somewhat by the length of the student's thumb. A shorter thumb will mean a lower arm. Also be sure that the left hand forms a C-shape as though holding a glass of water. Do not let the base knuckles collapse in toward the neck.

- **Bass tip:** Notice the suggested fingering in measure 2 and 3 where bassists stay in III position across the D and G strings. Isolate these measures before playing the entire piece.

**3.23 TUNING ETUDE** **Vln./Vla.** *Are all your Gs in tune? How about 4th finger A?*

**Cello** *Are all your Gs in tune?*

**Bass** *Are all your Gs in tune? How about your As?*

**THEORY**

# UPBEATS

**Upbeats** (pick-up notes) lead into the first full measure of a phrase. When upbeats are used
to begin a piece, their combined rhythmic value is often subtracted from the last measure.

## UPBEAT | RETAKE

- Demonstrate bow placement for the upbeat. Students often
  think it has to be at the tip, but it can start just above the middle
  of the bow or a bit closer to the tip. Try both placements and
  have students listen to and evaluate the results.
- To help the first note speak clearly, a little bow weight may
  be necessary to grab the string, especially if the students
  begin closer to the tip.

- Review retakes (bow lifts) with students. Be sure the bow has
  landed securely back on the string before pulling the second
  down-bow.

## 3.24 DRY BONES *An upbeat is often played with an up bow!*

Spiritual

SB307TM

## VIOLIN
### NEW NOTE: B

B is played with 2 fingers on the G string.

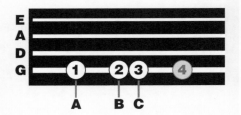

## VIOLA
### NEW NOTE: B

B is played with 2 fingers on the G string.

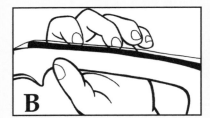

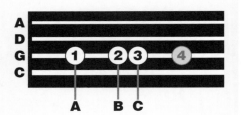

## CELLO
### NEW NOTE: B

B is played with 3 fingers on the G string.

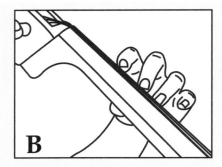

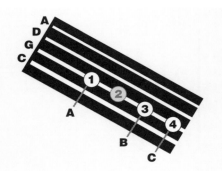

## DOUBLE BASS
### NEW NOTE: B

B is played with 1 finger down on the A string.

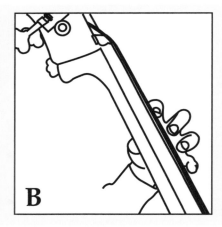

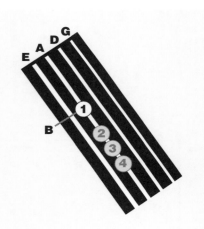

**NEW NOTE: B**

- Listen for good intonation on the new note. If intonation is an issue, have students start on the open string and add fingers.
  Play G, then A, then B. Basses play A, then B.

## 3.25 B-WARE

**REINFORCING B | RETAKE**

- Continue to reinforce that the retake is a continuous motion. Students should lift the bow in a single, counter-clockwise semicircle and set it back down gently in the same place they started.

## 3.26 RAIN, RAIN, GO AWAY Vln./Vla. *Make a tunnel over the D string with your 2nd finger only. This will prepare you for the next piece!*

Traditional

- Isolate measure 1 so students can practice fingered string crossings. Practice slowly at first, so students can focus on moving just one finger to the other string.

- **Extension:** Demonstrate a slow, heavy bow to represent the heavy oars and big boat. Show the students that, in this case, bow weight is more important than bow speed. See if the students can add some weight from the arm as well as the right-hand 1st finger. A strong, bent thumb will secure the heavy bow arm.

**3.27 VOLGA BOATMEN** Vln./Vla. *Put your 2nd finger on the G string. Prepare for your 1st finger on the D string.*
**Cello** *Put your 2nd and 3rd fingers on the G string. Prepare for your 1st finger on the D string.*

Russian Folk Song

## COMBINING A AND B WITH D STRING NOTES

- Remind students to look ahead in the music and prepare their fingers, especially when they are playing open strings.
- Demonstrate the first measure using quick strokes on the eighth notes and fast bows on the quarter notes. Have students echo back in the same manner on open D or the D scale. After helping them keep their bows straight, practice the quarter note measures. Tie them together and experiment with short vs. long quarter notes. Which ones do the students like best?

- **Extension:** Can students imagine how a chicken on a fence post would look and move? Ask them to play the music so that it sounds like the pictures in their minds. Tell students it is okay to relax and move their bodies to the music (within limits!).

## 3.28 CHICKEN ON THE FENCE POST

American Folk Song

## VIOLIN
### NEW NOTE: C

C is played with 3 fingers on the G string.

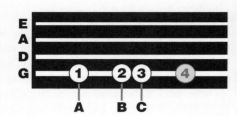

## VIOLA
### NEW NOTE: C

C is played with 3 fingers on the G string.

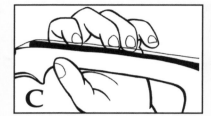

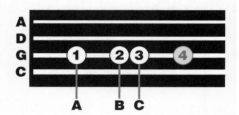

## CELLO
### NEW NOTE: C

C is played with 4 fingers on the G string.

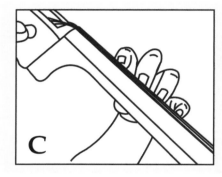

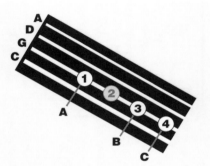

## DOUBLE BASS
### NEW NOTE: C

C is played with 2 fingers down on the A string.

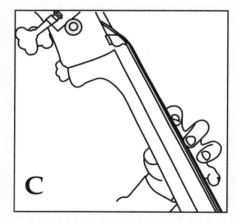

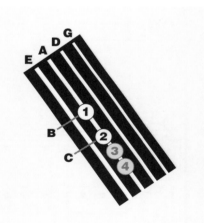

## New Note: C | G Tetrachord

- Before playing this exercise, it may be helpful for students to begin on an open string and play up to the note C. Remind students to keep firm left-hand weight on the string.
- Once violins, violas and celli have established the tetrachord, have all students practice going from open string to the C.

- Demonstrate a slow, heavy bow on last note of the piece.
  - As the contact point moves above the middle of the bow and into the upper half, students must add arm weight to maintain consistent volume.
- **Violin / Viola tip:** Make sure the 4th finger hovers over the string. Constantly address any fingers that are curling up.

## 3.29 DOWNS AND UPS

## Reinforcing C | Preparing the G Major Scale

- Students should be subdividing all half notes so they receive full value. Encourage them to think "slow bow" for each half note.

## 3.30 JUST ABOUT THERE...

SB307TM

# NEW KEY SIGNATURE

This is the key of **G Major.**  This key signature indicates that all Fs should be played as F-sharps.

## G MAJOR KEY SIGNATURE | G MAJOR SCALE

- Ask students what is different about the G Major key signature compared to D Major.
- Demonstrate the finger pattern for a one-octave major scale. Remind the students all notes are one alphabet letter (or step) apart. Review which scale degrees are whole steps and which are half steps. Demonstrate measure by measure.

- Bassists should play this in first position before shifting (if teachers / students choose to shift into II position).

## 3.31 G MAJOR SCALE

G MAJOR | REINFORCING C

- **Violin / Viola tip:** Leave the 1st finger down on the D while setting the 3rd finger on the G in measure 2.
- **Cello tip:** Leave the 1st finger down on the D and have fingers 2, 3, and 4 land together on the G string in measure 2.

- **Bass tip:** Sneak finger 2 across to the A string while finger 1 remains on the D string in measure 2
- The eighth notes can be played in a bouncy and fun style. Demonstrate the piece and ask students if it sounds like a galop.

## 3.32 GALOP

**The following information appears in the violin and viola books.**

## 4th-FINGER D (ON THE G STRING)

Use 4th-finger D for smoother technique and a richer sound in appropriate places.
You can check your intonation by comparing it to your open D.

4TH-FINGER D (VIOLIN / VIOLA) | G MAJOR | RETAKE

- **Violin / Viola tip:** Check that left elbows are well under the instrument. Remember that pulling the elbow to the right will help bring the 4th finger right over the G string!

- Encourage students to use the lift at the end of measure 4 to prepare left-hand position for the note C.

**3.33 LITTLE DUCKLINGS** Vln./Vla. *Intonation check! Are your Ds in measure 2 in tune?*

German Folk Song

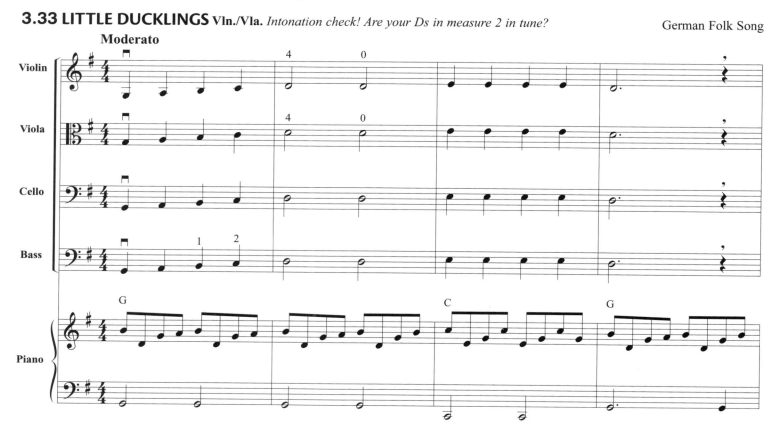

RHYTHM

**TIE**

A **tie** is a curved line that connects notes of the **same pitch.** These notes are bowed together and played to sound like one longer note.

- Reinforce that two tied quarter notes of the same pitch are played exactly like one half note. Demonstrate how the bow does not change direction between the tied notes.

## 3.34 GIVE IT A TIE

RHYTHM

## SLUR

A **slur** is a curved line that connects notes of **different pitches.**
Slurred notes are played **using a single bow.**

- Reinforce the difference between slurs and ties. Ties connect notes of the same pitch. Slurs connect notes of different pitches.

- Reinforce how ties and slurs are played using a single bow.

### SLURS

- Demonstrate how to play two notes in one bow. Encourage students to keep the bow moving and follow the marked bowings. Keep that shark happy!

- Try to use the same amount of bow for each note within the slur; otherwise, students may clip the length of the second note in a slur. Students may need to play with slower bows so both quarter notes are full value.

## 3.35 HAPPY SHARK

### SLURS

- Demonstrate how to change bows (after the slur) without stopping the bow. Keep those waters smooth!

## 3.36 SMOOTH WATERS

## TIES

- Ask students to locate the three ties in the piece. Why are they ties and not slurs?

- This exercise prepares students for 3.38.

### 3.37 THREE TIED MICE

Adaptation

## SLURS

- Make sure students play a full value quarter note at the end of each slur. If they are clipping it, go back to 3.37 so students can focus on the bow stroke.

### 3.38 THREE GLIDING MICE

English Folk Song

- Demonstrate *legato* (smooth) bow changes. Look for straight bows, relaxed bow holds and smooth direction changes.

- **Cello tip:** Measure 2 would be a good place to try out 2nd position.

## 3.39 SLURS 'N' SCALES

## SLURRING EIGHTH NOTES

- Make sure students play a full value eighth note at the end of each slur. The note should connect into beat 3.

## 3.40 A BOW A BEAT

- Help students play both *legato* and *maestoso* with balanced posture and straight bows. Discuss what makes a melody beautiful.

- **Cello tip:** For the motivated cellist, using second position can help make a more mature sound. Be sure the left thumb stays relaxed. Have students clap for themselves with their thumbs!

- **Bass tip:** Students should play this piece in first position before practicing the optional shifts.

- **Extension:** For variations, students might try playing *Ode to Sleep* or *Ode to Scariness* and discover how changing their bow speed, length or pressure can make this piece less joyful. After experimenting, students can put the joy back into it!

**3.41 ODE TO JOY** Cello *Bow-nus! Shift to 2nd position where indicated!*                    Ludwig van Beethoven
              Bass *Bow-nus! Practice playing this piece using both* II *and* III *position as indicated.*
              *Your teacher may suggest another option as well!*

## MUSIC

Austrian composer **Gustav Mahler** (1860–1911) is best known for his large symphonies. He spent time in New York conducting both the Metropolitan Opera and the New York Philharmonic. Ironically, his first symphony was not well received, and only became popular later.

## SCIENCE

Charles Darwin published his theory of evolution and described natural selection as a key mechanism. The Wright Brothers became famous when they built and flew an airplane using a control system they developed to help steer and maintain equilibrium.

## WORLD

In Canada, Banff National Park was established and became Canada's first national park. Things in the United States began to cool down when engineer Willis Carrier invented modern air conditioning!

### SLURRING EIGHTH NOTES | ROUND | MAHLER

- While playing each pair of slurred eighth notes, demonstrate how to count and move from the first note to the second note. Young players often have a tendency to rush into the second note.
- Isolate the last measure for all instruments so students can practice left-hand technique explained in the books (see below).

- **Violin / Viola / Cello tip:** On beat 3 of measure 5, encourage students to put their fingers down on the D string at the same time and in the correct pattern.
- **Extension:** Listen to a symphony orchestra recording of this movement. Which instrument plays the melody first?

## 3.42 THEME FROM SYMPHONY No. 1 - Round

Gustav Mahler

*Vln./Vla.* Keep your 1st and 2nd fingers down on their respective strings in the last two measures!

**Cello** *In the last two measures, keep your 1st finger down while fingers 2 and 3 go down on the G string*

**Bass** *Before playing, isolate the last two measures and practice "hopping" between strings.*

SLURS

- Practice clean, quick bow lifts where indicated.
- Isolate measure 14 (3 measures from the end) so students can practice the fast eighth notes and string crossing. If students need to, slow the passage down until it sounds clear and clean. Speed it up a little bit at a time.
- For fun, try it faster than notated, but keep the bow changes clean.

- **Bass tip:** As with many other similar exercises, have students play in 1st position before practicing notated shifts.
- **Extension:** William Billings was one of the first important American-born composers working in the late 1700s. *Chester* was such a popular hymn that it almost became the National Anthem!

## 3.43 CHESTER

William Billings

148

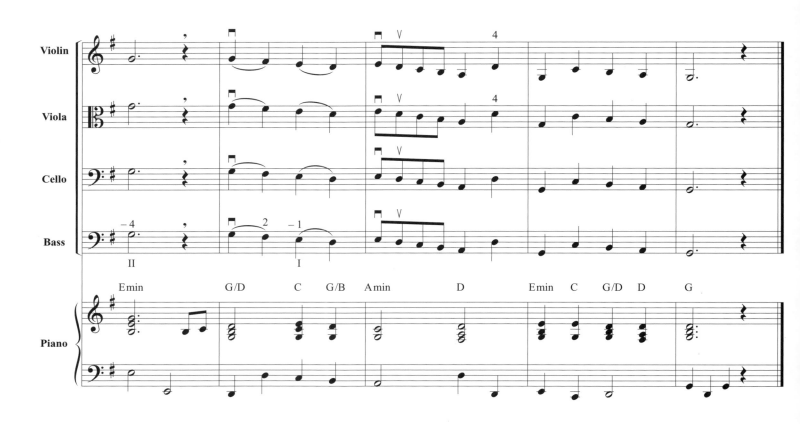

# OPUS 3 ENCORE

## INTERPRETATION STATION

*Interpretation Station* focuses on students' ability to listen to and make judgments about performance, style, expression, and contrasts.

- In this assessment, we focus on the student's ability to identify time signatures by ear. Students are always given a duple and triple meter choice (the authors do not ask to differentiate between 2/4 and 4/4). While designed as part of a unit assessment, this particular assessment can be used anytime.

- Students should listen to each example in class or at home and mark the correct answer in their book.

Listen to the corresponding track on the DVD. You will hear four musical examples, all composed using a different time signature. As you listen, pay close attention to how rhythmic ideas are grouped. Circle the correct time signature for each example.

1. **3/4   4/4**     2. **2/4   3/4**     3. **3/4   4/4**     4. **4/4   3/4**

**Answer Key:**   1. 4/4     2. 2/4     3. 3/4     4. 4/4

**Music:**   *Fanfare and Fireworks* – Brian Balmages

*The Bird* – Franz Joseph Haydn / arr. Matt Moreno

*Bagatelle* – Ludwig van Beethoven / arr. Carrie Lane Gruselle

*String Me Along* – Erik Morales

## SIMON SEZ

*Simon "Sez"* is an assessment of the development of aural skills. Performance skills gained from reading are discrete and different from performance skills guided by aural cues.

Below is a transcription of the familiar melody students hear on the DVD. Students, however, do not have anything in their books.

- Students can sing along at first to get the tune in their ear. Then they can experiment with finding the pitches on their instrument.

- Have students critique themselves and each other. *Did they match the recording?*

Listen to the corresponding track on the DVD. You will hear a well-known song. Listen first, sing it, then find the pitches on your instrument. You can then play along with the accompaniment track that follows!

# COMPOSER'S CORNER

*Composer's Corner* allows you to assess students' ability to transfer skills acquired from exercises specific to each Opus into a created product. It is a synthesis exercise to help you assess higher order thinking.

In this Opus, you learned about theme and variations. Take the following well-known melody and create your own variation.

## VARIATION ON TWINKLE, TWINKLE, LITTLE STAR

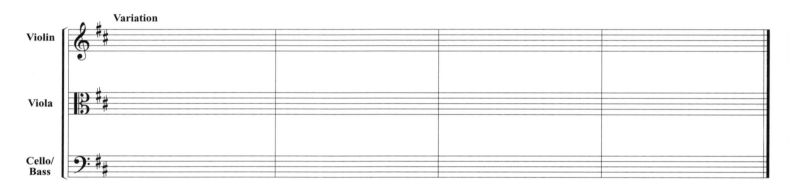

- Students may complete this particular assessment at any time during the Opus.
- Encourage students to perform their pieces for a partner, the class, or their family. Ask them which techniques they used to create a variation.

- Consider repeating the assessment as the students learn new notes and techniques.

## PENCIL POWER

*Pencil Power* assessments allow you to assess students' ability to identify certain musical concepts generally found in the written score. It also assesses broader musical knowledge.

Solve the following music math problems by notating the correct note value.

1. ♩ ⌣ ♩ = 𝅗𝅥

2. ♩. − ♩ = ♩

3. 𝅗𝅥 ⌣ ♩ = 𝅗𝅥.

4. 𝅗𝅥 − ♩ − ♪ = ♪

5. ♩ ⌣ ♩ ⌣ ♩ = 𝅗𝅥.

6. ♫♫ ⌣ = 𝅗𝅥

# CURTAIN UP!

The *Curtain Up!* section includes a performance piece covering material that has been reviewed in Opus 3. Students should be encouraged to use the DVD and give full performances for friends and family. This is also a time to learn performance and concert etiquette. Students should introduce the piece by its title and acknowledge applause by bowing.

## ASSESSMENT OF SKILLS PRESENTED IN OPUS 3

• Teachers should look for the following elements:

1. Proper playing position
2. Clean up-bow / understanding of upbeat
3. Slurs
4. Understanding of 1st and 2nd endings
5. Use of 4th finger

6. Bow hold
7. Bow stroke
8. Left-hand fingers are curved and wrist is straight
9. Bow distribution on half notes
10. Understanding of tempo marking

**3.44 THE MOREEN** *When you see **enclosed repeat signs** (‖: :‖), repeat the music between the signs (do not go back to the very beginning!).*

Irish Air

The *Bow-nus!* section focuses on bow technique. This is an ideal time to offer extra credit and further right-hand development. Encourage students to use the same bow stroke in measure 4 as they are doing in measures 1-3. It may be helpful for them to think "slo-wer bow" while connecting the three notes.

THREE NOTES IN ONE BOW

**3.45 SERENADE FOR STRINGS** *Practice slurring three notes in one bow!*

Pyotr I. Tchaikovsky

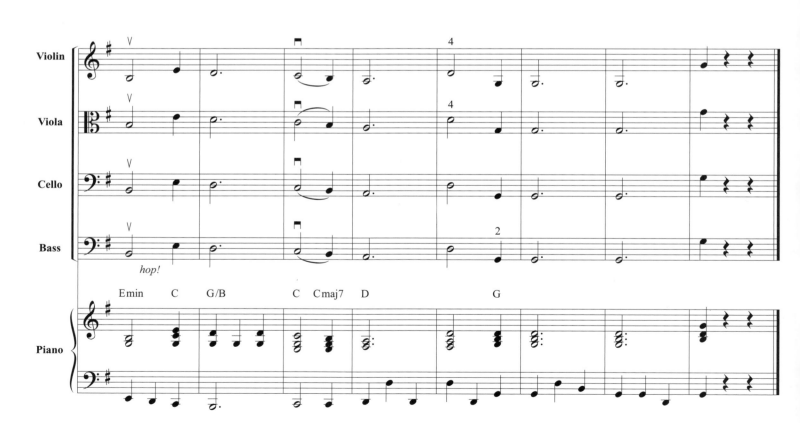

# CURTAIN UP!

- All orchestra arrangements include A, B and C parts.
  - A = melody
  - B = harmony
  - C = bass line

- All instruments contain the A line. Violin and viola also have the B (harmony) line while cello and bass have the C (bass) line.

- Students should not use too much bow on the eighth notes. Pulling and pushing a lot of bow on these notes can slow the group down and cause the bow to simply slide back and forth on the surface of the string.

- Demonstrate a thin sounding, bow sliding on the surface tone. Show students how a little weight added from the right hand or arm can keep the sound lively and full on the eighth notes.

## 3.46 FANTASTIC FIDDLES - Orchestra Arrangement

Brian Balmages

154

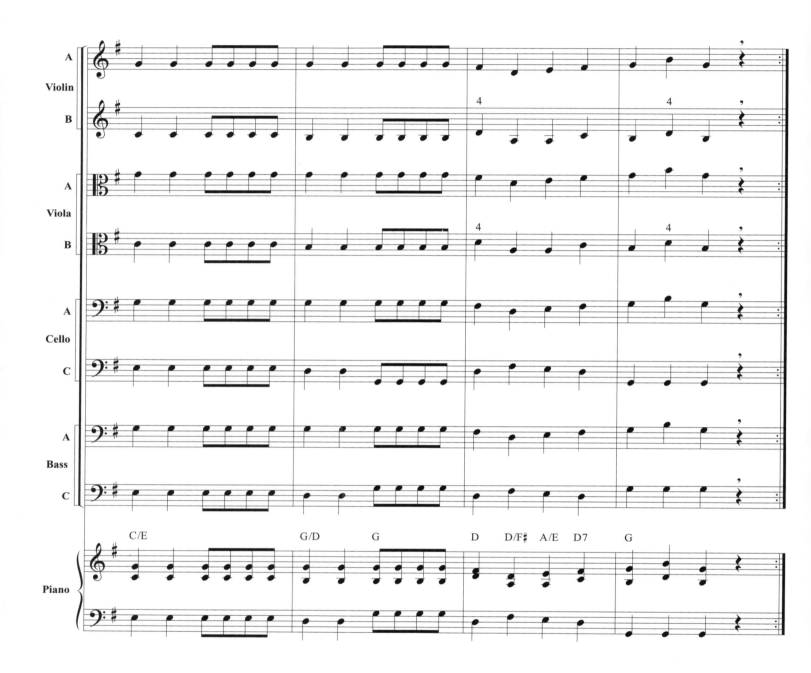

- Practice playing the piece together before dividing students into groups. Be sure all students get an opportunity to be in group 1 and group 2 (add a group 3 if you would like!).

**3.47 DO YOU HEAR? - Round** Cello *Bow-nus! Shift to 2nd position where indicated!*

French Folk Song

- Ask the students to read and think about the composer's note. A demonstration might be in order to reveal exactly how the teacher makes this happen. A key to success is to lighten up on the up bow. Use a bit less bow and bow speed on up bows compared with down bows. This may be one of those times that a demonstration of the wrong way (stressing the up-bow) will make it easier to understand.

## 3.48 PRELUDIUM (After J.S. Bach) - Orchestra Arrangement

Brian Balmages

*With your bow, stress the first beat of each measure to achieve the proper style.*

# OPUS 4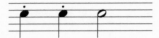

## STACCATO

**Staccato:** Play short and separated by stopping the bow between notes.

### STACCATO

- Ask students to stop the bow quickly and lift the arm weight (but not the bow) quickly and gently to get a clean release. Practice this with individual bow strokes until students are comfortable.

- Pressing the hairs too firmly into the string may result in a less than pleasant sound.

- Flexibility in the right-hand fingers will help staccato notes sound natural and not forced. It will also allow students to adjust for subtle differences in dynamics and phrasing.

- Make the contact point near or above the balance point, depending on the dynamics. Cellos and basses will have the contact point closer to the balance point.

- Refining this technique will allow you to see if students are keeping their fingers reasonably relaxed.

## BASS

**Reminder: Most exercises that use second position can also be played in first position!**

## 4.1 SHORT AND SWEET

STACCATO | DUET

- Staccato bow strokes are generally thought of as belonging in the upper half of the bow for violin and viola and at the balance point for cello and bass.
- Have the students start each down bow near the middle or balance point. Be sure everyone understands there are two elements to staccato notes:
    1. The previously mentioned separation or space between the notes.
    2. A little "pinch" from the right-hand first finger before any staccato note. How much pressing and how fast to draw the bow depends on the dynamic and context. A good demonstration from the teacher will make it relatively easy to teach.

- The teacher can play the A part and the class can play the B part. Students can echo you and imitate your staccato.

## 4.2 DUELING CUCKOOS - Duet

# DYNAMICS

**Dynamics** indicate how loudly or softly to play. Italian terms are often used in music to indicate volume.

***p*** *(piano)* – play softly          ***f*** *(forte)* – play loudly

## DYNAMICS | STACCATO

- Decide whether you want students to stop the bow on the string after the quarter note and then make a quick lift and recover for a new down bow, or just lift as a follow through to the quarter and then recover.

- **Extension:** The dynamics between measures 1 and 2, then measures 3 and 4 allow students to play the *piano* right where the bow stopped after the *forte* quarter note. Learning to do this without lifting the bow can help avoid unwanted bow noise in more advanced music.

## 4.3 ECHO ETUDE

**DYNAMICS | STACCATO | MISTERIOSO**

- Discuss the definition of *misterioso*. What techniques can students use to achieve this style?
- Stress playing the opening in the upper half of the bow (violin / viola) or in the middle (cello / bass), gradually sneaking back closer to the frog just before the *forte*. After all, this is a sneaky tune! Lift and recover back to the frog for the "Boo!"

- Remind students that there are only 5 beats of *forte* in the entire piece.
- Help them avoid playing the staccato quarter notes too loudly after playing the four eighth notes.

## 4.4 SPOOKY GHOSTS AND GOBLINS

# HOOKED BOWING

Play both notes in the same bow direction, stopping the bow between each note.

## HOOKED BOWING | DYNAMICS

- Demonstrate the pattern by rote, using open strings. This will help students understand how much separation you prefer. A few echo patterns on open strings can be very helpful before playing notated music.

- Some students may instinctively grip the bow tightly on the hook. To avoid that, see if they can feel how to make the bow weight lighter on the string.

## 4.5 HOOK 'EM!

- Discuss the definition of *allegretto*. Make time to play a recording of the symphony, particularly this movement. It is never too early for students to be inspired by great music (You may consider playing it as students enter the room). Ask students how it would feel if the music was slowed down to *Moderato* or sped up to *Allegro*.

- **Extension:** this may be a good time to introduce playing a little closer to the fingerboard than the bridge to get a gentle, but still clear sound.
- When the class is playing as a duet, are both parts playing with the same style?

## 4.6 ALLEGRETTO FROM SYMPHONY No. 7 - Duet

Ludwig van Beethoven

**Allegretto** (*a tempo between moderato and allegro*)

HISTORY

### MUSIC

Austrian composer **Wolfgang Amadeus Mozart** (1756–1791) was a child prodigy and composed his first minuet when he was just five years old! In his short 35-year life, he wrote over 600 musical compositions that are still performed today.

### SCIENCE

French chemist Antoine Lavoisier recognized and named oxygen. He also wrote the first extensive list of elements and helped develop the metric system. He is widely considered to be the "Father of Modern Chemistry."

### WORLD

The thirteen American Colonies issued the *Declaration of Independence,* a statement that justified the American Revolutionary War against Great Britain. The document was approved on July 2nd, but not formally adopted until July 4th, which became Independence Day.

### HOOKED BOWING WITH HALF AND QUARTER NOTES

- Read about Mozart and what was happening in the rest of the world while he was composing.
- Demonstrate how to slow the bow speed down for the half notes; use less bow and do not let it go too far into the lower half.
- Encourage students to play non-marked quarter notes *legato* for contrast.

- You can introduce students to phrasing in this piece. What ideas do they have for making this musical?
- Make time to play a recording of the actual sonata. It is never too early for students to be inspired by great music (Again, if time is an issue, consider playing it as students are entering the room.)

## 4.7 THEME FROM SONATA No. 11

Wolfgang Amadeus Mozart

**Cello** *Bow-nus! Play this entirely on the D string by shifting to 2nd position where indicated.*
**Bass** *While this piece can be played entirely in* I *position, using* II *and* III *position helps eliminate string crossings and makes the piece sound more musical.*

- Demonstrate the arm motions. You may want students to practice the string crossing arm motions without the bow.

- Even though students are moving to adjacent strings, remind them that they require only minimal raising and lowering of the arm.

## 4.8 CRISSCROSS APPLESAUCE

SLURRING ACROSS STRINGS

- Exercise 4.8 prepares students for the arm level change in 4.9. Have students play constant half notes to get a smooth, connected sound in their ears.

- Sing "smooth" on the slurs and "ride" on the half notes!

## 4.9 SMOOTH RIDE

- **Violin / Viola tip:** Point out how little the elbow (and thus the bow) has to change its plane.

- **Cello / Bass tip:** Students should keep the bow arm close to the upper string level rather than the D string level until the end of measure 3 (F♯).

## 4.10 UP, UP, AWAY

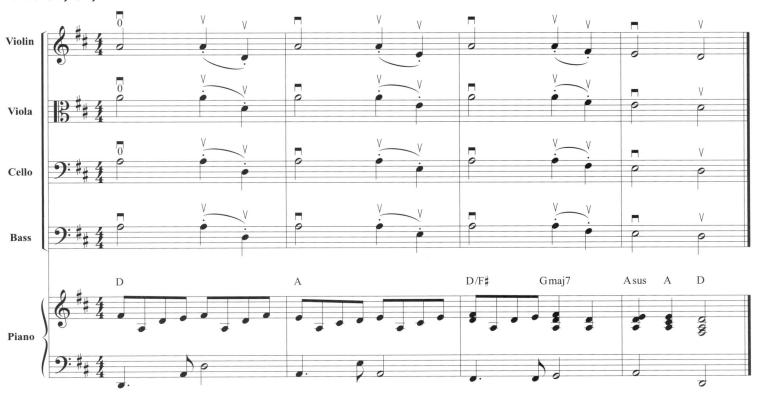

## SLURRING ACROSS STRINGS

If necessary, the teacher may demonstrate without the bow. As described in the opening of the book, isolating techniques such as the string crossing motion without sound can be useful to students.

## 4.11 BOW-DESTRIAN CROSSING

- Demonstrate and call attention to the rounded arc arm motion. Contrast by showing them a sudden, angular string crossing that would cause a bumpy seesaw ride.

### 4.12 SEESAW MUSIC  **Bass** *When slurring E and A, keep your 1st finger centered on E and lean your finger over to cover the A.*

ADDING FINGERS SLURRED STRING CROSSINGS

- Remind students about the rounded arc motion on the string crossings.

- Measure 4 sets up the opening measure in the following exercise, *Hush, Little Baby*. Make sure fingers are hovering over the string when not being used.

### 4.13 A LITTLE HERE, A LITTLE THERE

*Vln./Vla.* Have your 2nd finger hover over the C# in measure 4.
**Cello** Have your 2nd and 3rd fingers hover over the C# in measure 4.

- Introducing bassists to II½ position helps prepare them for exercise 4.14 and avoids crossing strings during a slur. 4.13a makes it quite easy to learn.

**SHIFTING**

## BASS
### SECOND AND A HALF (II½) POSITION

To play in **second and a half position**, shift your left hand so that your 1st finger moves to B on the G string. Remember that your thumb should also move, staying relaxed and behind your 2nd finger. You can now play C# with your 4th finger!

### 4.13a THE B TWINS - Basses Only *Practice shifting into and out of II½ position. Measures 1 and 2 should sound the same!*

- Discuss the definition of *dolce*. What can students do to make the music sound this way?
- Sing and model the *legato* sound of separate bows in measure 3. If you have not used the term legato yet, this would be a good time to do so and explain.

- Students may benefit from isolating the right hand and practicing the rhythm of this piece on an open string before playing the notated music.
- **Bass tip:** Isolate the first measure and have students play pizzicato. This may take a few attempts. Then isolate with the bow. This will help students feel more comfortable shifting within a slur.

**4.14 HUSH, LITTLE BABY** **Vln./Vla.** *Have your 2nd finger hover over the C♯ in measure 1.*     Traditional
                                  **Cello** *Have your 2nd and 3rd fingers hover over the C♯ in measure 1.*

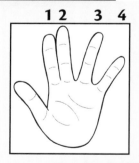

1 2   3   4

## VIOLIN
## LOW 2nd FINGER

Shape your hand as shown in the illustration. Notice that your 1st and 2nd fingers are now touching, and there is space between your 2nd and 3rd fingers. Keep this spacing when you move your hand to the fingerboard.

### C NATURAL

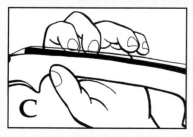

C is played with low 2 (low 2nd finger) on the A string

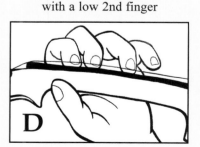

The fingering for D with a low 2nd finger

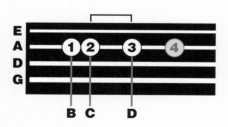

Notice the space between 2nd and 3rd fingers.

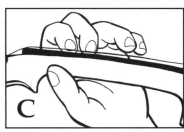

## VIOLA
## LOW 2nd FINGER

Shape your hand as shown in the illustration. Notice that your 1st and 2nd fingers are now touching, and there is space between your 2nd and 3rd fingers. Keep this spacing when you move your hand to the fingerboard.

## C NATURAL

C is played with low 2 (low 2nd finger) on the A string

The fingering for D with a low 2nd finger

Notice the space between 2nd and 3rd fingers.

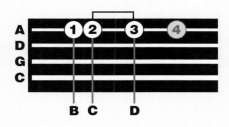

## CELLO
## C NATURAL

C is played with 2 fingers on the A string

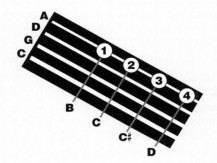

## BASS
## C NATURAL IN SECOND AND A HALF (II½) POSITION

C is played with 2 fingers on the G string in II½ position.

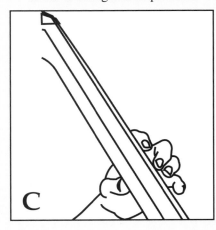

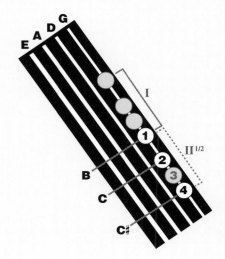

## ACCIDENTALS

A **natural** sign cancels a sharp or flat. It remains cancelled for the rest of the measure.

A **courtesy accidental** reminds you of a sharp, flat, or natural that already applies to a note.

SB307TM

• Measures 1 and 2 should sound identical. This is how bassists will know they found II¹/₂ position.

## 4.14a SHIFTING NATURALLY - Basses Only

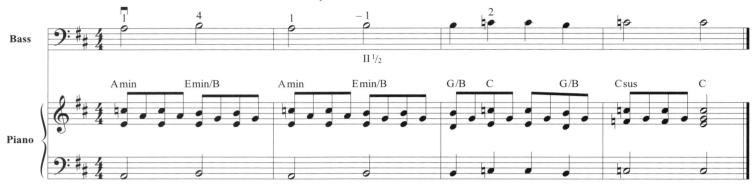

• When telling violins and violas about low 2nd finger, be sure the celli and basses realize this does not apply to them. Cello and bass players will not have their 1st and 2nd fingers as close together as on violin and viola.

• Spending sufficient time on this concept can help avoid the "low 2 blues" which can affect ensemble intonation.

• **Violin / Viola tip:** Many students struggle with low 2 because they are used to a finger pattern that uses high 2. These students often put their hand down and then slide their finger to low 2. This often results in poor intonation and technique. Use the following drop-and-lift technique as a guide to get students on the right track from the beginning. Consider  practicing this in both guitar and shoulder position.

  - Put down 1st finger on the A string  (B natural).
  - Move the side of the pad of the 2nd finger up against the 1st finger (just above the fingernail of the 1st finger).
  - Slide the 2nd finger down the side of the 1st finger until it reaches the string. It should still be touching the 1st finger, but now it is touching the tip of the 1st finger.
  - If you have students with very small fingers, they may need a *very slight* distance between the 1st and 2nd fingers. If you emphasize the aural concept along with the physical skill, as they grow, students should be able to adjust.

  - Students are now ready to play C natural on the A string.
  - After playing C natural a few times, have students slide the 2nd finger back up the 1st finger, to just above the fingernail.
  - Have students play B natural. It should still be in tune as the 1st finger should not have moved.
  - Do some echo patterns using B and C. Watch that the 2nd finger remains in light contact with the 1st. Some students will, from force of habit, stretch the 2nd finger away from the 1st and then slide it back. This is inefficient and teachers should reinforce the correct way of sliding an inch or so down and up the 1st finger.

• **Cello tip:** The 2nd finger is approximately halfway between 1st and 3rd finger.

• **Bass tip:** Students should find the first note of this exercise by playing up the scale from the G string.

  - They can also review 4.14a and stay in II 1/2 position to be ready.
  - They can test the C against the open G and listen for the perfect 4th (they can identify as the interval found in *Here Comes the Bride*).

## 4.15 LOW AND STEADY

- **Violin / Viola tip:** Go slowly at first. When students put down the 1st finger, they should let the 2nd finger drop into position with it (near the fingernail as described earlier). They will then be prepared to drop the 2nd finger onto the string. You may want to call this C natural "ready" position.
  - Students should prepare to stretch the 2nd finger up to C sharp (high 2) in the last 2 measures. Ideally, they should move the 2nd finger away when the 1st finger goes down in measure 3. That way it is in position and ready. You may want to practice this in guitar position.
  - When talking about 2nd finger placement, visual learners will find it helpful if you model placement every time it is mentioned in the early stages.

- It may be useful to have half the class play an open A string, while the other half plays either C natural or C sharp. Students will learn to listen for the minor or major third.
- **Cello / Bass tip:** This is a good opportunity to make sure left-hand fingers are arched and not collapsing at the knuckles.
- **Bass tip:** A review of 4.14a will help prepare students for the shift in measure 1.

**4.16 LOWS AND HIGHS** **Vln./Vla.** *High 2 (H2) reminds you that C♯ is played with high 2nd finger.*

The following exercise appears in the bass book and reinforces II¹/₂ position.

## 4.16a BLUES ETUDE - Basses Only *Practice shifting into and out of II¹/₂ position.*

# BASS
## C NATURAL IN THIRD (III) POSITION

C is played with 1 finger
on the G string in III position.

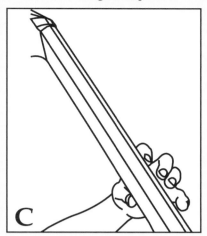

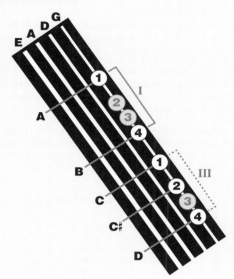

- Learning C natural in III position enables students to play C and D without switching positions.

The following three exercises help bassists to prepare for line 4.17. They reinforce C natural in both II½ and III position.

## 4.16b ALL THREE IN III - Basses Only

## 4.16c SHIFTING GEARS - Basses Only *As you shift, listen carefully to make sure your Bs and Cs match!*

## 4.16d C FROM I TO III - Basses Only

SB307TM

- **Violin / Viola tip:** Consider forming the finger pattern in guitar and shoulder position before playing. Inspect and correct each student. Then play a series of C naturals and Ds before playing the exercise, so students get used to the physical feel of the new finger placement.

- Draw attention to measure 3. Students may lower the 3rd finger along with the 2nd finger. If that happens, the octave Ds will not be in tune. Return to guitar position if necessary so students can feel (and see) the correct finger placement.

- Model and remind students to "pull and rotate" as they approach those 3rd fingers (pulling the elbow to the right, coupled with a slight rotation of the wrist to the left).

- **Cello tip:** Instruct students to place fingers 3 and 4 on the string together when playing the D following the C in measure 2. Beginning cellists will sometimes leave finger 3 above the string. This will cause tension in the hand and weaken the fourth finger. If your cellists used second position in Opus 3 (beginning on page 24), this will be the same finger pattern but now in first position.

- **Bass tip:** Remind students to keep all 4 fingers down while playing the open D in measure 3. Keep the left hand open and relaxed when moving between C and D.

### 4.17 DANSE HUMORESQUE Vln./Vla. *Are your octave Ds in tune? Make sure there is space between your 2nd and 3rd fingers.*

# REVISITING IMPORTANT LEFT-HAND POSITION TIPS FOR VIOLIN AND VIOLA

At this point in the method, students will begin combining left-hand finger patterns and hand shapes. It is important to review and reinforce the following information to ensure students develop a strong foundation. In addition, young students are constantly growing and it is easy for bad habits to get established, even if they were correct at one point. Continue to review the following information.

- Thumb placement: While one can find differences in thumb placement among skilled violinists, placing the pad of the thumb opposite the first finger is optimal for beginners. For example, it will facilitate later skills (especially shifting to higher positions).

- Point the thumb at the ceiling or possibly at a small angle. If the thumb straightens out and leans back toward the bottom of the scroll, this will start a trend that may end up with a "flat wrist," which should be avoided at all costs. Students with short thumbs may set the neck lower into the web between thumb and 1st finger to allow the latter to form that squared-off position that is so important to skills needed later. But do not let the tip of the thumb protrude above the fingerboard.

- While practicing C natural, many students curl up their 3rd and 4th fingers. Impress on them that this will make playing with those fingers more difficult, less in tune, and even impossible in fast passages. They must always hover above the string and not be curled out to the left of the hand. *The worst-case scenario is when any finger is curled beside the neck. This must be corrected immediately.*

- When violinists and violists play 3rd finger D, everything in the previous paragraph is applicable and important to the 4th finger. Refer to the drawings on page 36 often and have the students compare the drawn finger positions to their own.

- We often tell students to keep the elbow under the violin. Actually, we often need the elbow to swing farther to the right of the middle of the violin and a little closer to the player's belly button. An example is when your students are getting ready to use 3rd and 4th fingers. Another is when they play on the lower two strings, where a pull of the elbow to the right, coupled with a slight rotation of the wrist to the left pulls the 3rd and 4th fingers farther to the left, setting those fingertips in just the right place over the lower strings. Lead the class in modeling this swing of the elbow to the right while rotating the wrist slightly to the left without the instrument. When ready, do the same "pull and rotate" (toward the instrument) with the violin/viola in place, supported by the right hand if necessary.

- Demonstrate the two and finger patterns. Have students finger silently while you demonstrate, then play it pizzicato. Remind students not to let the 4th finger curl up (model right and wrong) and refer often to the drawing at the top of student page 36.
- Practice this exercise two measures at a time. Repeat each pattern several times, checking for all the skills they have studied in the previous three exercises. Then play the whole piece.

- Listen for accurate half steps and whole steps. Review finger placement, "drop and lift," and hand shape if necessary.
- **Cello tip:** Remind students that fingers 3 and 4 land simultaneously on the A string whenever a D follows a C natural.

**4.18 SHAPE SHIFTER** Vln./Vla. *This piece uses two different finger patterns (hand shapes). Isolate each pattern before playing them together.*
**Bass** *Pay close attention to where you use* II *and* III *position!*

COMBINING FINGER PATTERNS / HAND SHAPES

- **Violin / Viola tip:** Ask students to form the H2 finger pattern on the D string and check the octave pitch from the open G string to the 3rd finger G. Some students will grasp this pitch relationship quickly, while others will need the teacher's demonstrations and assistance. Adjusting and refining this octave pitch relationship is an important first step in training the ear to hear and perfect intervals.

  - If students do not get the 3rd finger G close enough to the 2nd finger F♯, show them how to place the 3rd finger up against the F♯ 2nd finger in a "ready" position and slide down to the string (as they did in the "ready" position for low 2nd finger).

- Spend time addressing the location of finger 3 when playing low 2. Often students will lower the 3rd finger when moving the 2nd finger to low 2. Watch to be sure students are placing the 3rd finger on the G and not creating an unintentional chromatic finger pattern (B-C-C♯).

## 4.19 DOODLE PRELUDE

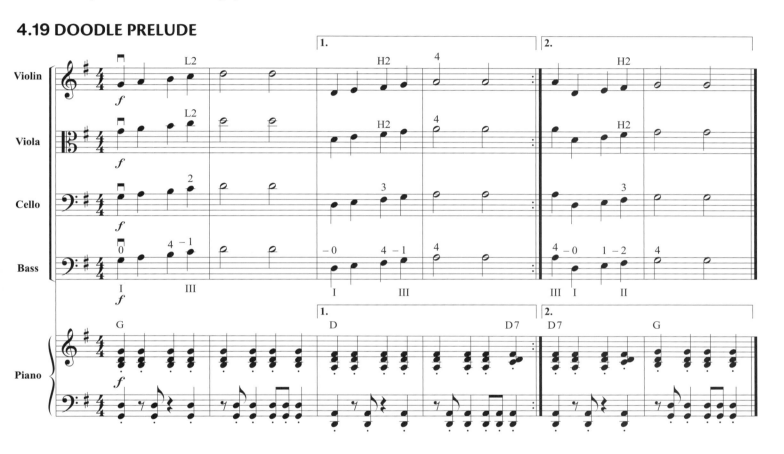

# BASS
## SECOND (II) POSITION ON THE G STRING

It is often ideal to use a position that requires the least amount of shifting. By using second position
in the exercises below, you will minimize the distance your hand must travel on the fingerboard while shifting!

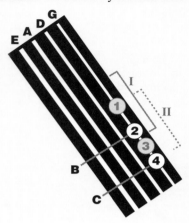

- Reinforce that it is often ideal to use a position that requires the least amount of shifting. By using II position, the hand does not have to travel as large a distance compared to II 1/2 or III.

## 4.19a CLOSER THAN YOU THINK - Basses Only *Listen to measures 1 and 2. They should sound the same!*

COMBINING FINGER PATTERNS / HAND SHAPES

- **Violin / Viola tip:** Some students will instinctively put all three fingers down on the D string in measures 1 and 2. Model how students can keep 1st finger on the A string and put only the 3rd finger down (or 2nd and 3rd fingers together). A similar situation happens 2 measures later when moving from B to G.

- **Cello tip:** Students should NOT put finger 4 down alone because it will weaken the hand frame.

**4.20 YANKEE DOODLE** **Cello** *Keep fingers down where indicated. Remember that fingers 2, 3, and 4 go down together while 1 stays on the A string.*

American Folk Song

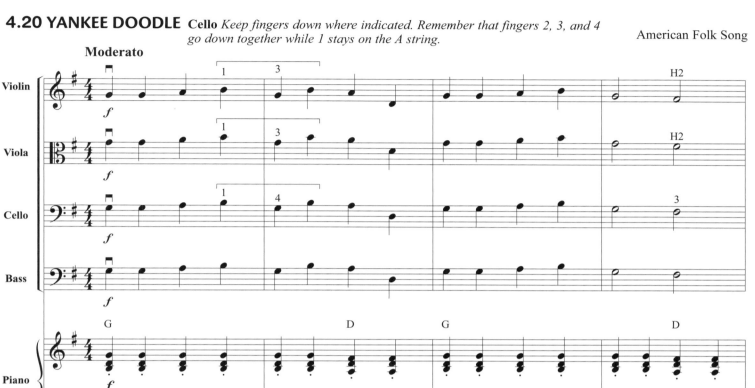

184

- This is a preparatory exercise for 4.21.
- Slowly play the first two notes and repeat until comfortable with shift. Gradually increase speed. Repeat the process going from D back to B (measure 1 into measure 2).

- Isolate all of measure 1 and repeat. Do the same for measure 2. Play the entire exercise.

## 4.20a SPEED SHIFTING - Basses Only *Practice shifting to* III *position quickly!*

### COMBINING FINGER PATTERNS / HAND SHAPES | HOOKED BOWING | SLURS

- Ask students to identify slurs and hooked bows. Isolate measures 1 and 3 so students can focus on technique.
- Demonstrate the hooked bows, showing how much separation there should be.
- Isolate measure 2. Show the class how to lighten up on the up bow stroke so it does not sound accented after the dotted half note.

- **Cello tip:** Be certain finger 3 is securely on the A string supporting finger 4 (not hovering over the string) after the C natural in measure 1.
- **Bass tip:** Practice the first three notes until they are fluid.

## 4.21 LA MORISQUE

Tielman Susato

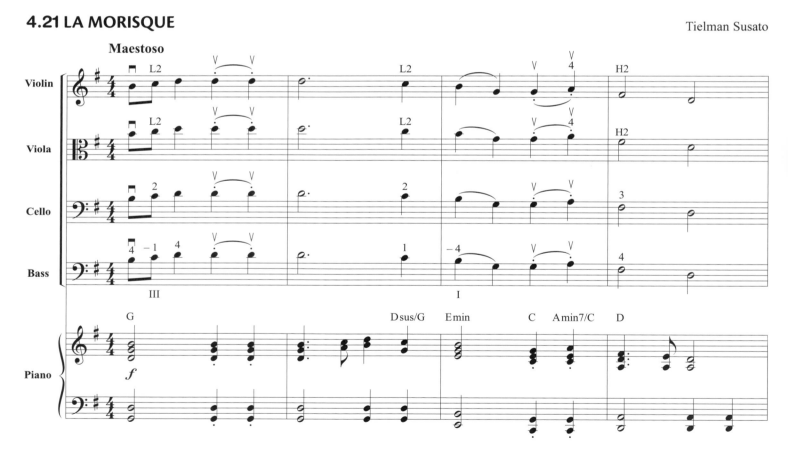

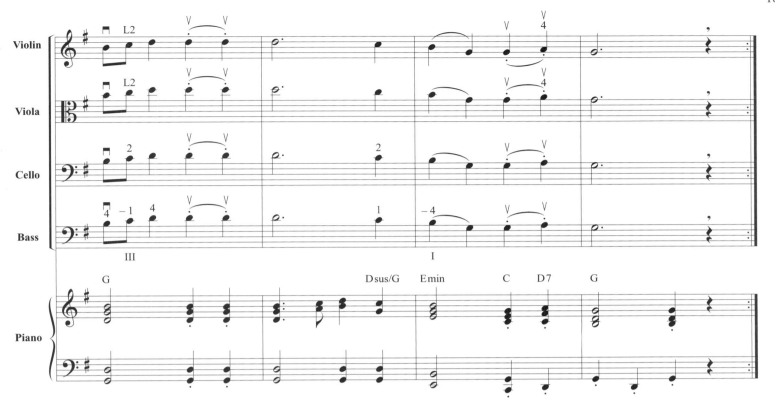

## COMBINING FINGER PATTERNS / HAND SHAPES | CLEAN STRING CROSSINGS

- Consider learning this piece two measures at a time.
- **Violin / Viola tip:** In the first two measures, work on a clean string crossing. In the next two, work on having the C natural in the "ready" position while playing the two B quarter notes. Remember to pull and rotate the left arm (toward the instrument) in preparation for 4th-finger A.

- **Cello tip:** This is a good time to check on left-hand thumb placement, ensuring it is behind / opposite the 2nd finger.

## 4.22 LOS POLLITOS

Mexican Folk Song

# BASS
## SECOND AND A HALF (II½) POSITION ON THE D STRING

To play second and a half position on the D string, move your 1st finger to F♯.
You can now play G with your 2nd finger!

**The following two exercises appear in the bass book and help prepare students for 4.23.**

### 4.22a SLIDING DOWN - Basses Only *Listen carefully, making sure your F♯s always match while you shift.*

### 4.22b PIECE OF CAKE - Basses Only *Notice how easy it is to shift between II½ and III position. Try playing measures 3 and 4 using I position instead of II½. Notice how much your hand has to move!*

# THEORY

# INTERVALS

An **interval** is the distance between two pitches. You can figure out the interval by counting each line and space between notes (include the first and last note). A **half step** is the smallest distance between two pitches. A **whole step** is the combination of two half steps.

## INTRODUCTION TO INTERVALS

- You may choose to start by introducing intervals via the D Major scale.
- Practice slowly, playing each measure two times.
- All students should listen for the octave Ds at the end of the study. Violinists and violists in particular need to be sure that finger 3 does not pull out of tune when in a low 2 finger pattern.

- **Violin / Viola tip:** When students move from C# to C natural, teach them to let the 2nd finger slide down into the low 2 position without actually coming away from the string. Do take the pressure off it, but maintain light contact with the string as the finger slides. They should not lift the finger and put it down again.
- **Cello tip:** For the interval of a 7th, students may leave fingers 2, 3, and 4 on the A string while the first finger plays the E.
- **Bass tip:** Review exercises 4.22a and 4.22b if students have any difficulty with this exercise.

## 4.23 ONE SMALL STEP...

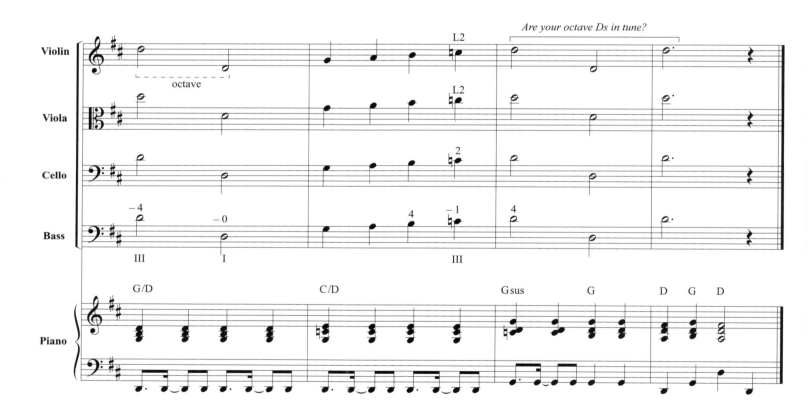

## VIOLIN
### NEW NOTE: F NATURAL

F is played with low 2
(low 2nd finger) on the D string.

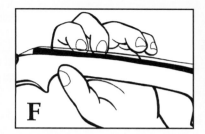

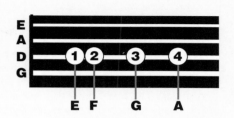

## VIOLA
### NEW NOTE: F NATURAL

F is played with low 2
(low 2nd finger) on the D string.

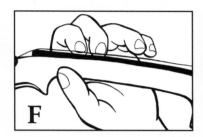

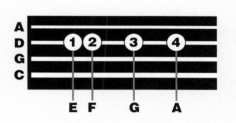

## CELLO
### NEW NOTE: F NATURAL

F is played with 2 fingers
on the D string.

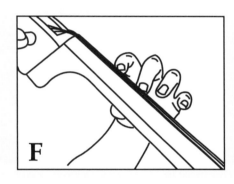

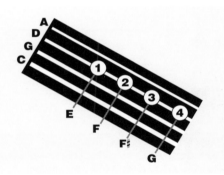

## BASS
### NEW NOTE: F NATURAL

F is played with 2 fingers
on the D string.

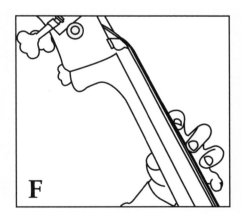

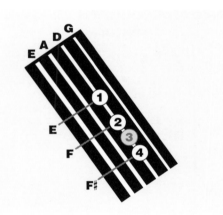

SB307TM

INTRODUCTION TO F NATURAL

- Relate this hand shape and finger pattern to C natural which they have already learned!
- **Violin / Viola tip:** While this exercise focuses primarily on the F natural, point out the left hand drawing at the top of the page. The third finger is stretched a whole step from the low 2nd finger. The tip of the 3rd finger is perched above the string, ready to drop directly in the right place.

- When telling violins and violas about low 2nd finger, be sure that the celli and basses realize this does not apply to them. Cello and bass players should not move their 1st and 2nd fingers closer together.

## 4.24 IT'S ONLY NATURAL

REINFORCING F NATURAL | MISTERIOSO | 2 UPBEATS

- Review *misterioso.* How can students play this piece to achieve that style?
- This is the first time students have seen a piece with 2 upbeats. Have them compare it with the last measure of the piece.

- **Violin / Viola tip:** It is a good idea to pull and rotate the left arm just before the 4th finger.
- **Cello / Bass tip:** Keep fingers 3 and 4 hovering over the string while playing F natural.

## 4.25 SNAKE CHANT *This piece has two upbeats.*

COMBINING F♯ AND F NATURAL

- **Violin / Viola tip:** The 2nd finger never completely loses contact with the string as it slides. It simply lets up its pressure and slides quickly in coordination with the bow change.

- **Bass tip:** Put fingers 3 and 4 down together when changing from F natural to F sharp. Remember to keep all fingers down when playing finger 4.

### 4.26 SLIDER
**Vln./Vla**. *Slide your 2nd finger to move between L2 and H2.*
**Bass** *Keep your hand open and relaxed when playing F♯ in this exercise.*

- For best results, start slowly to establish correct finger movements studied earlier on the page. Gradually increase speed. Use a quick and fairly long bow stroke on the eighth notes. This will force students to play the first two eighth notes lower in the bow (LH = lower half) or at least low in the balance point. The next two eighth notes are played fairly high in the bow (UH = upper half). Play with energy in the right arm and quick finger movement in the left. Have fun! Go for the Galop!

**4.27 LOW-HIGH GALOP** Bass C# *is played with 4 fingers on the A string.* (Errata – note that early versions of the bass book incorrectly refer to the G string here.)

REINFORCING F NATURAL | PESANTE

- Discuss the term *pesante*. Ask students to use a heavy (but not too slow) bow for the *pesante* sound.
- Go for a serious, weighty texture with help from the right arm while maintaining correct position.

- In measure 3, leave the 1st finger on the D string until the C that follows is sounding.

## 4.28 DIES IRAE

attr. Thomas of Celano

**THEORY**

# NEW KEY SIGNATURE

This is the key of **C Major**.

This key signature indicates all notes are played natural (no sharps or flats).

C MAJOR | REINFORCING F NATURAL | HOOKED BOWING

- **Violin / Viola tip:** Check to see that low 2 fingers are touching 1st fingers.

- **Bass tip:** It will take some practice to get the two up bows in measure 7 because of the leap from G string to E string. Motivated students can play measures 7 and 8 entirely in II position (low G uses finger 1 and that finger then hops to the A string to play the last note). This results in a skip of one string instead of two.

## 4.29 SHEPHERD'S HEY *Is your octave in tune in measure 7?*

English Folk Song

- Once students are successful, consider playing a new rhythm and have students echo various rhythm or bow patterns on each note of the scale.

## 4.30 C MAJOR SCALE

- For variety, consider making a dynamic change on the repeat.

## 4.31 COUNTRY GARDENS

English Folk Song

- The quarter note in measure four is an upbeat just like the one at the beginning. It should sound the same even though it is hooked from the half note.
- The upbeat does not need to start at the tip. Students will have more bow control if they start a few inches above the middle of the bow.

- **Violin / Viola tip:** Check that students are pulling the elbow well under the instrument. The left wrist should be slightly rotated toward the instrument and pulling the fingers toward the G string.
- **Cello / Bass tip:** Students should be in the lower half of the bow throughout this piece.

### 4.32 THE MAN ON THE FLYING TRAPEZE

Vln./Vla./Cello *Prepare for the A in measure 3!*
Bass *Prepare to hop in measure 1, where the second finger hops from the E string to the A string.*

Gaston Lyle

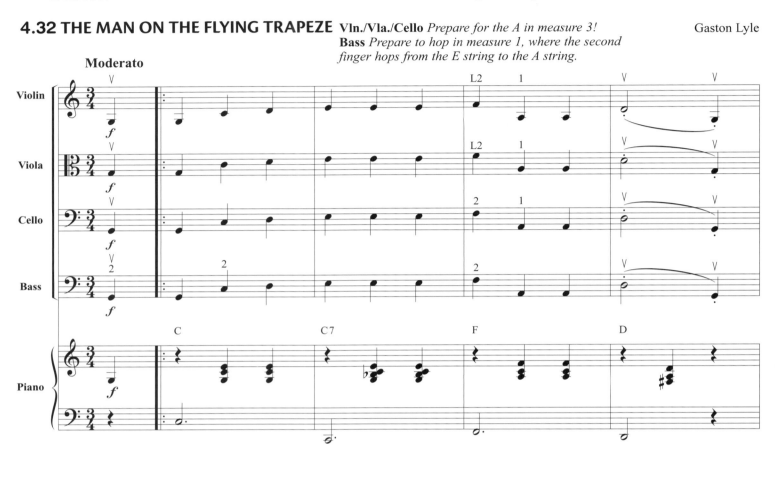

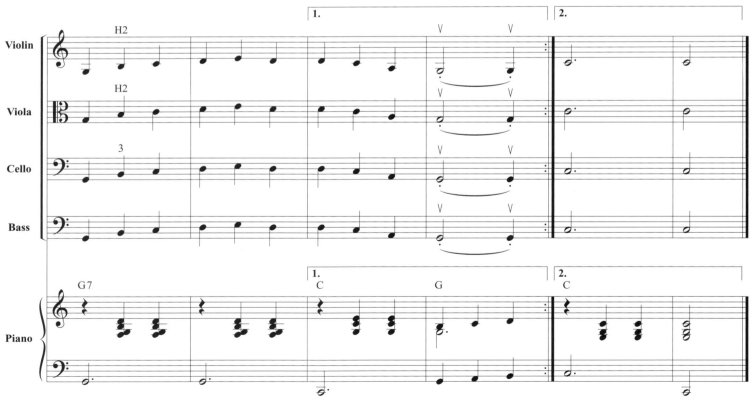

Slurs | C Major

- Reinforce student book instructions for playing smooth slurs, especially in measure 1.
- A fast, light bow stroke will result in a tender, gentle tone quality.

- **Bass tip:** Practice the first measure by slurring from open A to open D, then from open D to open G. Once students are comfortable, add fingerings.

## 4.33 THEME FROM HANSEL AND GRETEL

Engelbert Humperdinck

**Vln./Vla.** *For smoother technique, keep 2nd and 3rd fingers down where indicated.*
**Cello** *For smoother technique, keep fingers 3 and 4 down while preparing fingers 1 and 2 on the A string.*

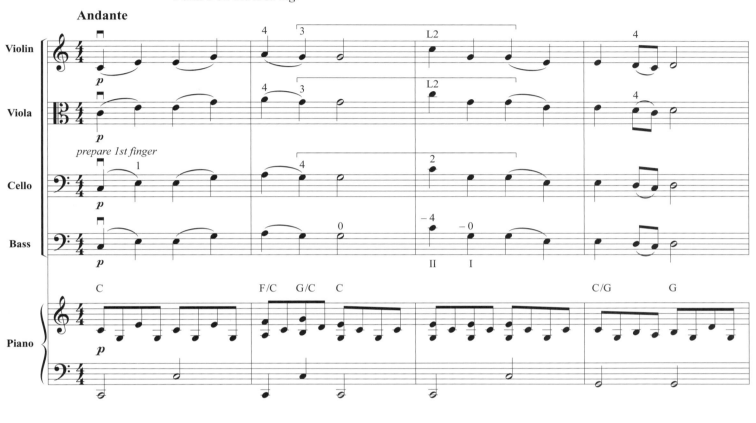

- Identify the five notes that make up this piece. Write it on the board and have students play the notes in order ascending and descending.

- **Bass tip:** Motivated students can practice this without using the open G string.

**4.34 FLOWER DRUM SONG** Cello *Put fingers 3 and 4 down at the same time.*

Chinese Folk Song

## WHOLE REST

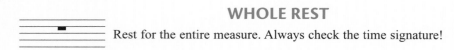

Rest for the entire measure. Always check the time signature!

**In this method, violists and cellists learn notes on their C string at the same time violinists and bassists learn notes on their E string. This keeps things fresh and exciting for the entire class.**

## VIOLIN
### NOTES ON THE E STRING

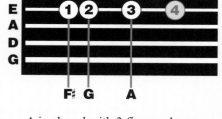

F♯ is played with 1 finger down

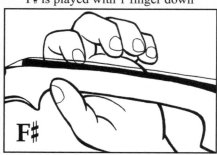

G is played with low 2nd finger

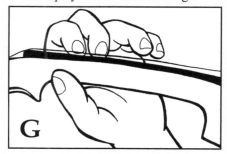

A is played with 3 fingers down

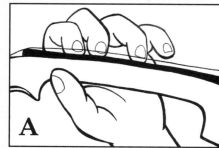

## VIOLA
### NOTES ON THE C STRING

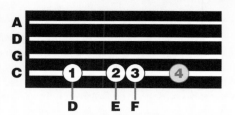

D is played with 1 finger down

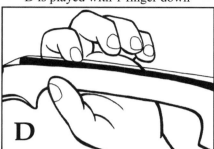

E is played with low 2nd finger

F is played with 3 fingers down

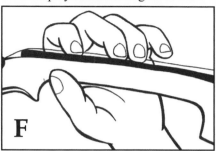

## CELLO
### NOTES ON THE C STRING

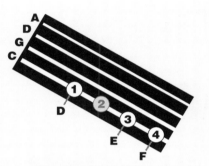

D is played with 1 finger down

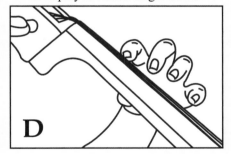

E is played with 3 fingers down

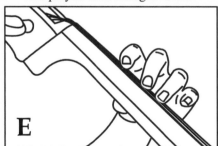

F is played with 4 fingers down

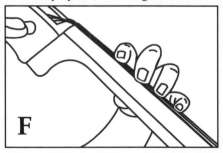

## BASS
### MORE NOTES ON THE E STRING

F♯ is played with 1 finger down
on the E string.

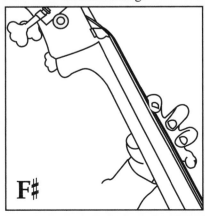

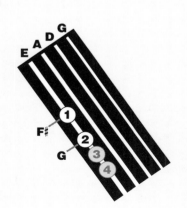

- Violinists can demonstrate the brighter, stronger sound of the open E string by playing it with the bow a little closer to the bridge than usual.
- All other instruments will need to use a heavier arm and bow a bit closer to the frog when engaging their lowest strings.

- **Cello tip:** Students should use the lower half of the bow.
- **Bass tip:** Students should be instructed to use less bow on lower pitches and remain in the lower half of the bow

## 4.35 E BATTLES C

**NEW NOTE: D (Viola and Cello) | NEW NOTE: F♯ (Violin and Bass)**

- Reinforce bowing tips presented in exercise 4.35.

## 4.36 GALACTIC MISSION

NEW NOTE: E (VIOLA AND CELLO) | NEW NOTE: G (VIOLIN)

• Reinforce that violinists must play this G using low 2nd finger.

## 4.37 ROCKIN' TO THE E.G.

- **Violin / Viola tip:** When students put three fingers down, remind them that the 4th finger should also hover over the string (and not curl up next to the neck!).

## 4.38 BROKEN BEETHOVEN BLUES

- Demonstrate bow management with the upbeat. Avoid starting at the tip with a fast bow which makes an unwanted accent, but a slow bow keeps the whole song in the upper half where the tone is too weak. A demonstration is probably the fastest way to show how to manage the bow for a strong, resonant sound throughout.

- **Viola tip:** Students can challenge themselves to play all Gs with 4th finger even though it is not marked until measure 7. The left elbow needs be pulled toward their D or A string in order to easily reach the C string.

- **Cello tip:** Have students add weight to their right index finger and have a strong, bent right thumb to produce a solid tone on the C string in measure 1.

- **Bass tip:** Motivated students can practice this piece without any open G strings.

### 4.39 A-TISKET, A-TASKET  Vla. *In measure 7, play your low G using 4th finger on your C string.*

American Folk Song

**HISTORY**

## MUSIC

**Franz Schubert** (1797–1828) was an Austrian composer who wrote over 600 pieces in his short 32-year lifespan. His *Marche Militaire* was originally written for piano four-hands (2 people playing one piano), but has since been arranged for virtually every type of performing ensemble.

## SCIENCE

Louis Agassiz was a Swiss paleontologist who became the first to scientifically suggest the presence of an ice age in Earth's history. He became a leading figure in the study of natural history.

## WORLD

A Russian expedition discovered Antarctica in 1820. Years later, Charles Wilkes discovered that it was not just an island, but a whole continent!

## VIOLA
### NEW NOTE: E

E is played with 4 fingers on the A string.

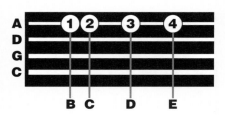

---

**4TH-FINGER E** (VIOLIN AND VIOLA) | **SCHUBERT** | **HOOKED BOWING** | **STACCATO**

- Read about Schubert and other world events occurring at the same time he was composing.
- In the opening 8 measures, encourage students to make the hooked quarter notes sound the same as regular staccato quarter notes. Young players have a tendency to make hooked staccato notes short and choppy.

- Students should sustain the half notes *forte* for their full value (no diminuendo in the upper half). Show them how to make a contrast with the *piano* section really soft and even a little playful sounding, while the *forte* response is strong and resonant.

### 4.40 MARCHE MILITAIRE Vln. / Vla. *In this piece, play your upper E using 4th finger on your A string.*

Franz Schubert

## VIOLIN
### NEW NOTE: B

B is played with 4 fingers on the E string.

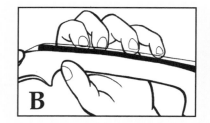

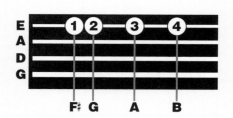

F♯  G  A  B

---

NEW NOTE: B (VIOLIN)

- Observe dynamics to make it dramatic!

- **Violin / Viola tip:** Students should strive to make the 4th-finger tone as clear and bright as the other notes. Remind them to "pull and rotate" the left arm and wrist slightly to bring them into position with strength.

## 4.41 UP AND AT 'EM!

- Students may need to practice this slowly at first, gradually speeding up the tempo as they are able.

## 4.42 TURKISH MARCH

**Moderato**

Wolfgang Amadeus Mozart

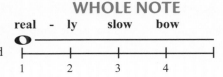

## WHOLE NOTE

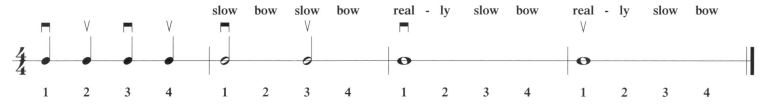

**Whole Note**
4 beats of sound

Use a really slow bow
when playing whole notes!

## WHOLE NOTE

- Model the various bow speeds while reciting the words above the notes.
- Remind all students that longer notes offer different challenges. In addition to counting, it is important to sustain a nice tone throughout the note.
- Have half the class play quarter notes as the other half plays whole notes. Switch.

- **Extension:** To make whole notes seem more attainable, play the "how many beats can you hold the note?" game. The teacher holds it for 16 or 20 beats and the students try to beat the record!

## 4.43 BOW BEAT *Rosin (tube) bow.*

## REINFORCING WHOLE NOTES

- Have students compare this rhythm with 4.43.
- While the quarter and half notes can be played around the middle of the bow, show students how to manage the bow so that the first whole note begins near the frog and the second begins near the tip. Cellists and bassists may use a shorter, heavier bow stroke than the upper strings.

- This exercise allows a whole bow for each of the whole notes. Consider teaching about bow weight, speed and contact point by playing this exercise both *piano* and *forte*. Point out that *forte* half notes can be played by using a fast bow or a slow bow. The slower bow requires greater weight to keep the sound strong.
- Remind students to count "1-2-3-4-off" in the last measure so they do not cut off when they get to beat 4.

## 4.44 THE OH-SO-SLOW BOW TO GO

# DYNAMICS

**Crescendo** means to gradually play louder.

**Decrescendo** means to gradually play softer.

- Practice crescendos and decrescendos on an open string first. Then consider applying to a scale or tetrachord (crescendo up and decrescendo down).

- Apply the elements of bow management from the previous exercise. Play slowly at first so students can think about and apply weight, speed and contact point adjustments, all of which change quickly in this melody.

## 4.45 CONCERTO THEME

Ludwig van Beethoven

**HISTORY**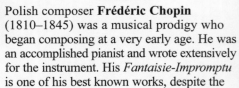

## MUSIC

Polish composer **Frédéric Chopin** (1810–1845) was a musical prodigy who began composing at a very early age. He was an accomplished pianist and wrote extensively for the instrument. His *Fantaisie-Impromptu* is one of his best known works, despite the fact he never wanted it to be published!

## SCIENCE

In 1842, Christian Doppler, an Austrian physicist, proposed what became known as the Doppler effect. It explained why the pitch of a police siren changed as it approached and passed an observer.

## WORLD

In 1836, the Texas Revolution ended when the Republic of Texas was established after a year-long revolution against Mexico. In 1845, it became the 28th state in the U.S.

CHOPIN | DYNAMICS | BOW SPEED

- Read about Chopin and what was happening around the world while he was composing.
- Reinforce bow speed, weight and contact point, and a sustained, singing sound.

- **Extension:** Can anyone in the class explain how a solo piano could play the dynamics in the second measure?

**4.46 FANTAISIE-IMPROMPTU** *Notice how the tie connects the E in measure 4 to measure 5, making it last 4 beats.*

Frédéric Chopin

# OPUS 4 ENCORE

## INTERPRETATION STATION

*Interpretation Station* focuses on students' ability to listen to and make judgments about performance, style, expression, and contrasts.

- In this assessment, we focus on students' ability to identify tempo and style markings by ear. While designed as part of a unit assessment, this particular assessment can be used anytime after line 4.28.

- Students should listen to each example in class or at home and mark the correct answer in their book.

Listen to the corresponding track on the DVD. For each example, choose the style or tempo marking that best fits the music.

| | | | | | | |
|---|---|---|---|---|---|---|
| 1. | Andante | Allegro | | 3. | Maestoso | Misterioso |
| 2. | Pesante | Dolce | | 4. | Allegro | Moderato |

**Answer Key:** 1. Andante    2. Pesante    3. Misterioso    4. Allegro

**Music:** *A Beethoven Lullaby* – Brian Balmages
*Afterburn* – Brian Balmages
*Ghost Lights* – Timothy Loest
*Allegro barbaro* – Béla Bartók / arr. Bob Lipton

## SIMON SEZ

*Simon "Sez"* is an assessment of the development of aural skills. Performance skills gained from reading are discrete and different from performance skills guided by aural cues.

Below is a transcription of the familiar melody students hear on the DVD. Students, however, do not have anything in their books.

- Students can sing along at first to get the tune in their ear. Then they can experiment with finding the pitches on their instrument.

- Have students critique themselves and each other. *Did they match the recording?*

Listen to the corresponding track on the DVD. You will hear a well-known song. Listen first, sing it, then find the pitches on your instrument. You can then play along with the accompaniment track that follows!

# COMPOSER'S CORNER

*Composer's Corner* allows you to assess students' ability to transfer skills acquired from exercises specific to each Opus into a created product. It is a synthesis exercise to help you assess higher order thinking. In this case, it deals with basic improvisation in a safe environment where students will feel successful.

**Improvisation** occurs when a performer makes up music on the spot without any previous preparation or written music. Experiment with the guide notes. You can then have a friend or group play the accompaniment line while you improvise (or you can play along with the accompaniment track). *Note: The recording is played 4 times.*

**Guide Notes**

## "ATTITUDE" - Accompaniment Duet

- Students can play this assessment while other students play the duet or they can play along with the accompaniment track provided on the DVD or online.
- Students may feel more comfortable starting with just one or two notes and focus on rhythm. As they become more comfortable improvising, they can add additional notes.
- Consider repeating the assessment as students learn new notes and techniques.

## PENCIL POWER

*Pencil Power* assessments allow you to assess students' ability to identify certain musical concepts generally found in the written score. It also assesses broader musical knowledge.

- Students may complete this assessment in class or at home. The teacher can decide whether this should be an open or closed book assessment.

Match the composer with the correct fact by writing in the appropriate letter.

1. _____ Tchaikovsky    **5.** _____ Beethoven

2. _____ Mahler    **6.** _____ Handel

3. _____ Schubert    **7.** _____ Mozart

4. _____ Chopin

A. Continued to compose music after becoming completely deaf
B. Accomplished pianist who also wrote extensively for piano
C. Austrian composer who wrote *Marche Militaire*
D. Child prodigy who composed his first minuet when he was 5 years old
E. German composer who was hired to write music for fireworks in London
F. Composer known for his symphonies who was equally at home as a conductor
G. Russian composer of *The Nutcracker*

**Answer Key:**   1. G    2. F    3. C    4. B    5. A    6. E    7. D

## CURTAIN UP!

The *Curtain Up!* section includes a performance piece covering material that has been covered in Opus 4. Students should be encouraged to use the CD and give full performances for friends and family. This is also a time to learn performance and concert etiquette. Students should introduce the piece by its title and acknowledge applause by bowing.

### ASSESSMENT OF SKILLS PRESENTED IN OPUS 4

- Challenge your students to have a strong and consistent tone throughout each whole note. This will require adding bow weight as they move toward the tip, and relaxing weight as they move toward the frog.

- Teachers should look for the following elements:
  1. Proper playing position
  2. Bow distribution on whole notes
  3. Use of 4th finger
  4. Bow hold
  5. Bow stroke
  6. Left-hand fingers are curved and wrist is straight
  7. Even sounding slurs
  8. Understanding of style marking

### 4.47 THE GREAT GATE OF KIEV *Practice playing with a full bow and project a big, beautiful sound!*

Modest Mussorgsky

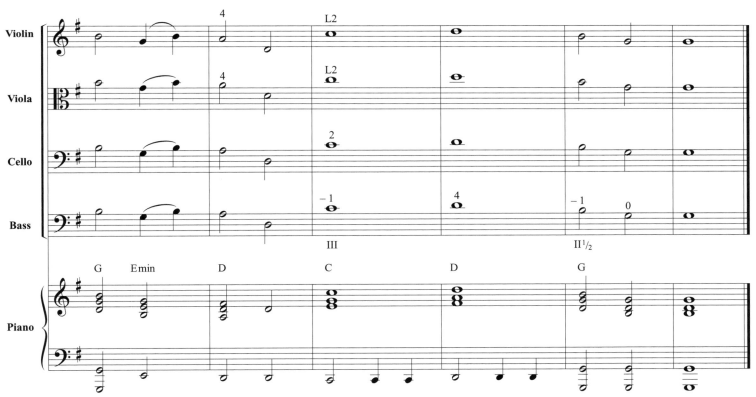

# CURTAIN UP!

- All orchestra arrangements include A, B and C parts.
  - A = melody
  - B = harmony
  - C = bass line

- In measures 1 through 8, quarter notes should be somewhat short. Keep a steady beat, using eighth notes as the pulse. In measures 9 through 15, exaggerate the dynamic contrasts by using a very long bow (not too long for the basses) for *forte,* and short, light bows for *piano.*

- All instruments contain the A line. Violin and viola also have the B (harmony) line while cello and bass have the C (bass) line. As these arrangements become slightly more intricate, there are brief moments when the violin B line differs from the viola B line.

- Students should track the entire road map of the piece, marking repeat signs, first, and second endings.

## 4.48 CAN-CAN - Orchestra Arrangement
### (from "Orpheus in the Underworld")

Jacques Offenbach
arr. Carrie Lane Gruselle

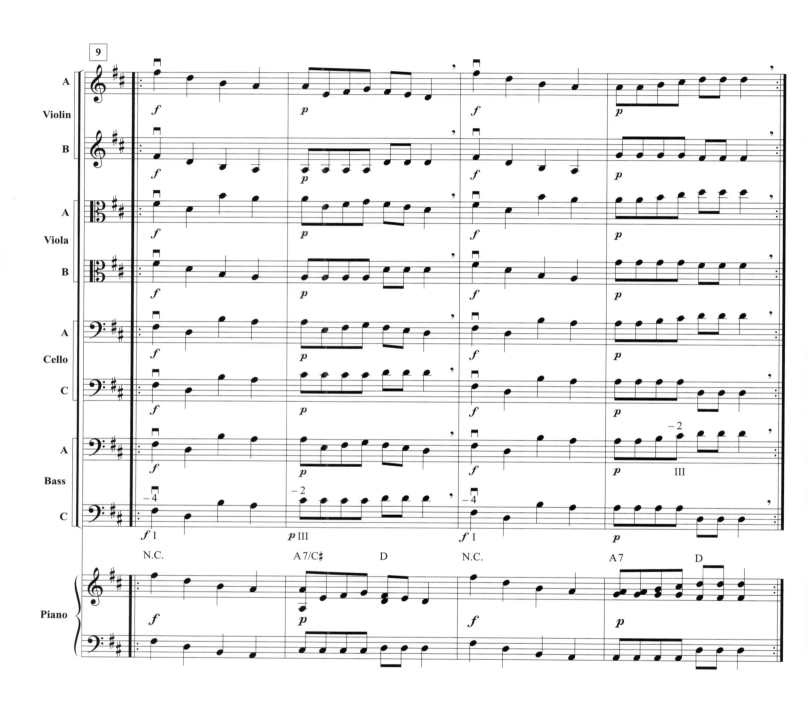

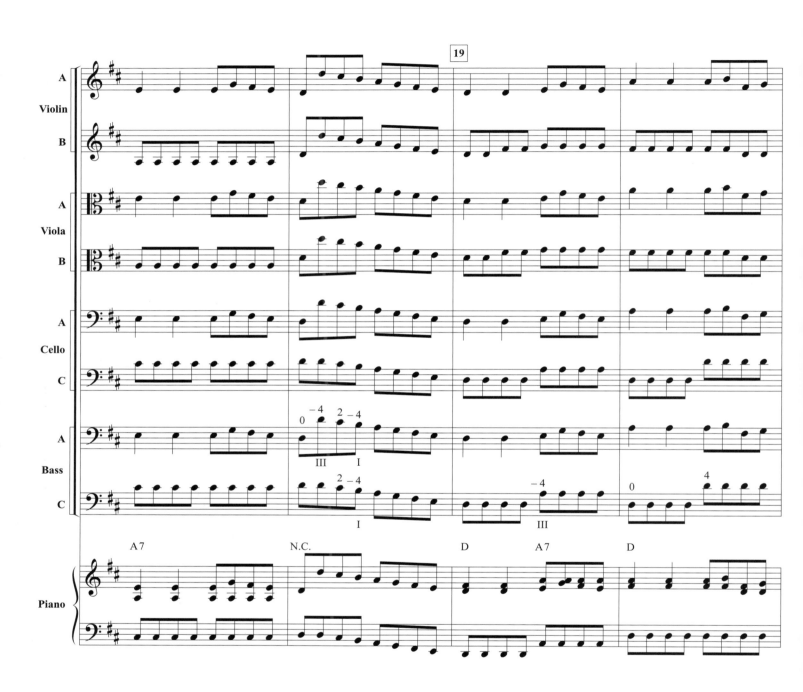

# CURTAIN UP!

- Up bows need to sound as powerful as down bows. Use weight from the arm rather than leaning the hand slightly on the index finger. A good test to see if up and down bows match is to reverse the bowings!

- Students should track the entire road map of the piece before playing. Mark repeat signs, *D.C. al Fine,* and *Fine.*

## 4.49 POWER AND PULSE - Orchestra Arrangement

Brian Balmages

An instrument-specific solo is provided in all student books and includes a piano accompaniment part for performance. Students may also play along with the accompaniment track provided. Note that piano accompaniment tracks are separate from the demonstration track for easy use in performance should a pianist not be available.

# INSTRUMENTAL SOLO - VIOLIN

**4.50 MINUET AND TRIO - Solo**

Franz Joseph Haydn
arr. Brian Balmages

**Piano Accompaniment**

SB307TM

# INSTRUMENTAL SOLO - VIOLA

**4.50 PETIT RONDO - Solo**

Jean-Nicolas Geoffroy
arr. Brian Balmages

## Piano Accompaniment

# INSTRUMENTAL SOLO - CELLO

**4.50 A ROCOCO THEME - Solo** *Bow-nus! Use 2nd position where indicated!*

Pyotr I. Tchaikovsky
arr. Brian Balmages

**Piano Accompaniment**

SB307TM

# INSTRUMENTAL SOLO - BASS

**4.50 SONATINA - Solo**

Cornelius Gurlitt
arr. Brian Balmages

**Piano Accompaniment**

# SCALES AND ARPEGGIOS

**THEORY**

## ARPEGGIO

An **arpeggio** is the first, third, and fifth notes of a major scale played in succession. It may also include the 8th scale note (an octave above the starting note).

Practice each scale using the rhythmic patterns below for each note. Your teacher may suggest additional patterns. Try making up your own!

**1.** **2.** **3.** **4.** **5.** **6.**

### D MAJOR

### G MAJOR

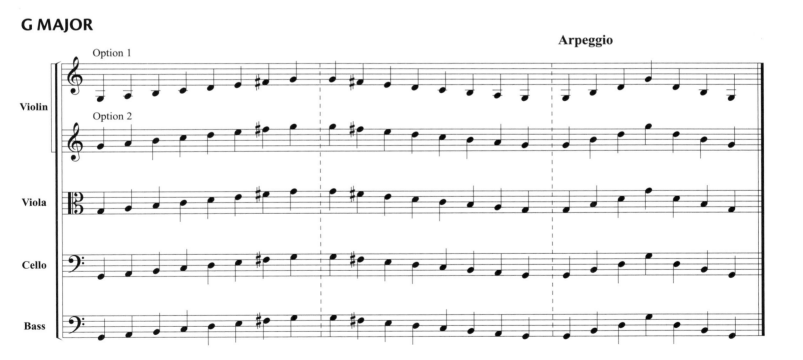

# SCALES AND ARPEGGIOS

**C MAJOR**

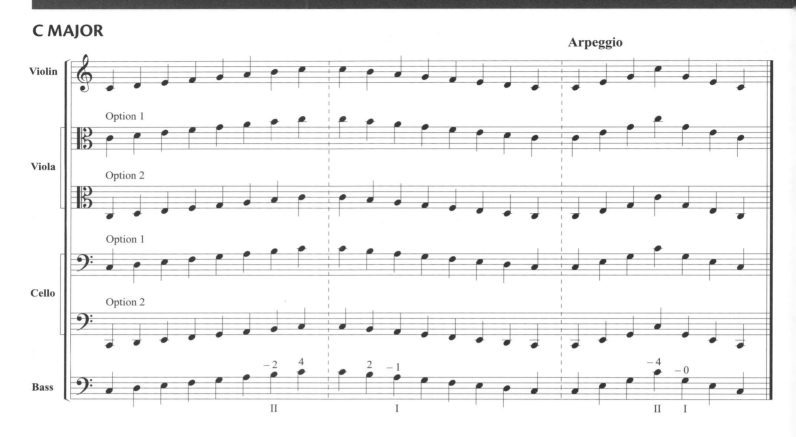

# SCALES STUDIES - Basses Only

**4.51 D MAJOR STUDY** *Make sure your thumb is relaxed and stays behind your 2nd finger when you shift.*

**4.52 G MAJOR STUDY**

**4.53 C MAJOR STUDY**

# POSITION STUDIES FOR BASS

Page 47b of the bass book is dedicated to position studies. These studies are organized by position so students can focus in on specific techniques. The last study combines all the positions they have learned in Book 1 and is an excellent challenge for the motivated bassist.

## I/III POSITION STUDIES

### 4.54 STUDY No. 1

### 4.55 STUDY No. 2

## I/II POSITION STUDIES

### 4.56 STUDY No. 1

### 4.57 STUDY No. 2

## I/II½ POSITION STUDIES

### 4.58 STUDY No. 1

### 4.59 STUDY No. 2

## MIXED POSITION STUDY

### 4.60 SHIFTING ETUDE

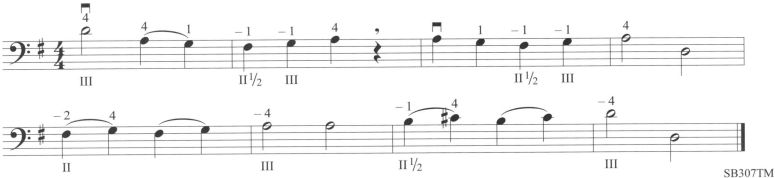

# VIOLIN FINGERING CHART

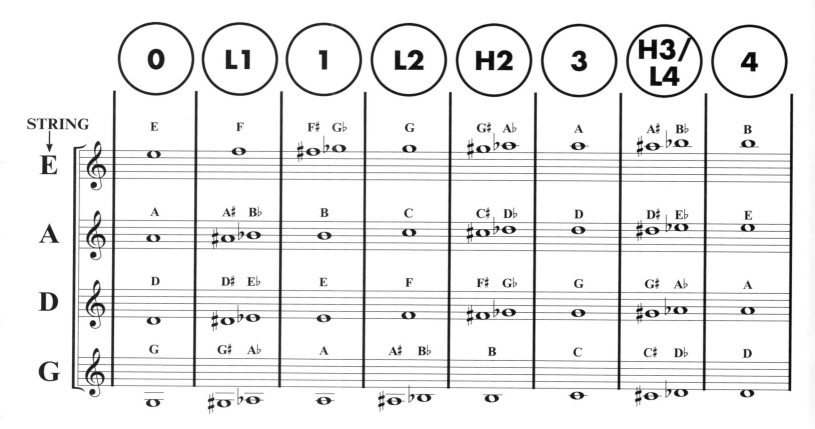

# VIOLA FINGERING CHART

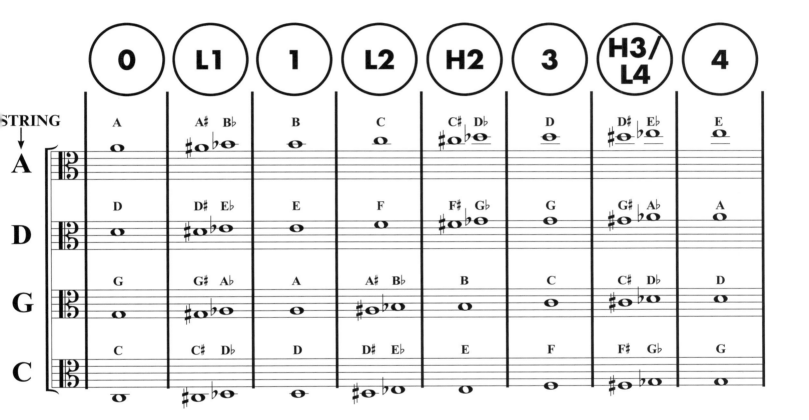

# CELLO FINGERING CHART

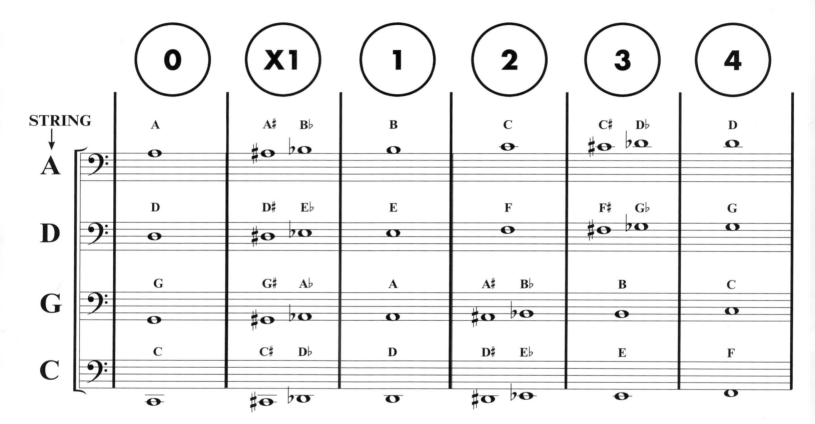

# BASS FINGERING CHART

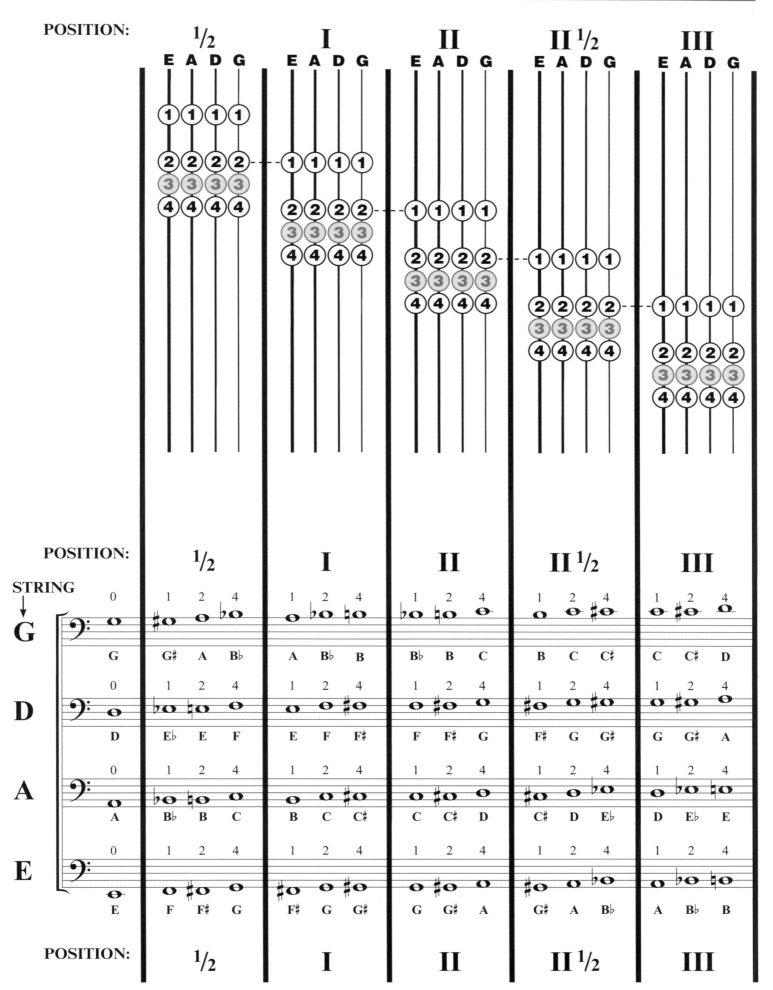

# INDEX